BEHIND THE CURTAINS

Thomas P E Wells

To all the important people: essential for my life's recovery and its purpose.

Copyright and confidentiality warning ©

The information, ideas and concepts, and the expression of them (together the "Confidential Material") disclosed in the attached draft are confidential and are disclosed by Dr Tom Wells for publication of Dr Tom Wells' story, Behind the Curtains, only (the "Permitted Purpose"). In consideration of Dr Tom Wells' supply (verbal or written) of the Confidential Material, you undertake not to disseminate, copy or use the Confidential Material other than for the Permitted Purpose without Dr Tom Wells' prior written permission. Dr Tom Wells claims all copyright and other intellectual property rights which vest whether now or in the future in the Confidential Material.

Copy 11, 222 pages
Dr Thomas Peter Edward Wells
19 February 2008

ISBN 978-1-84799-664-0

CONTENTS

Author's prologue: setting the scene.
1. 16 March 1992: the unforgiving slippery slope of accidental change.
2. Ghosts of a former life: my childhood.
3. September 1988 to March 1992: medical school in London prior to the accident.
4. The first ten days: French hospital.
5. Return to home ground.
6. Frenchay hospital: visitors, hallucinations, jaw plates, back rods, breathing difficulty and another moment to change my life forever.
7. Odstock: the journey down.
8. Odstock: arrival, impressions and initial progress.
9. Odstock: further progress.
10. When did I realise that I had been badly and permanently injured?
11. Raising money: a past challenge of mine achieved by others; generosity abounds.
12. A trip to Salisbury in the Spinal Injuries Unit minibus.
13. Further trips outside.
14. A night in the adapted self-contained flat of the Spinal Injuries Unit.
15. A trip back home.
16. What did the first weekend home entail?
17. Where was I going to live when I left hospital?
18. Unplanned neck operation: the tracheal scar tissue lives.
19. Legal challenges.
20. Odstock: influential people.
21. Assessment for tracheal reconstruction.
22. Tracheal reconstruction.
23. Vocal at last and hoisted by nurses.
24. December 1992: a hospital Christmas.
25. The wrong tube or the wrong neck?
26. Did the holiday insurance pay up? What was the excuse now?
27. How did the retrial in France go?
28. What was my future? Medicine wanted and a tale of two cities.

29 First proper assessment since the major throat operation.
30 16 March: a good or a bad day?
31 June 1993: released from the hospital, still much to be achieved.
32 Later in June 1993: second throat assessment since the main operation.
33 How did I move on after such a bad accident?
34 Holiday with family in Cornwall.
35 September 1993: return to medical school.
36 Learning to do the doctor bit as a student.
37 October 1993: throat lasering; third time lucky?
38 When would the operations stop?
39 Physical pain is an issue.
40 Comic moments: condoms, toilet issues and strange people.
41 Further holidays: viva España in the main.
42 Outside interests: cinema, fitness and photography.
43 Philadelphia: the pain was not mine this time.
44 What a weekend! My left foot, casualty and imminent medical exams.
45 Results of finals: dad had to do the deed.
46 August 1996: transition from student to actual doctor.
47 Further medical exams.
48 A voyage to remember: sun, calm sea, sea urchin spikes, two Norwegians and a broken front wheel.
49 Now how did I get out of this dreadful mess?
50 Where am I now?
51 Closing thoughts: the end is near.

Author's prologue: setting the scene

Tom Wells was a student doctor in London, when a devastating event happened that was to have a radical effect on his life. He was involved in a tobogganing accident, when on a skiing holiday in France. Within a second, his life was changed forever. He sustained multiple injuries, including spinal cord injury, chest trauma, jaw fractures, brain injury and some more. Having survived his initial injuries, he had to contend with paralysis and the inability to speak, due to windpipe narrowing resulting from a tracheostomy tube procedure performed a few days after the accident. A wheelchair was to be a permanent feature of his life but, fortunately, he regained his speech after several operations.

    This is his story of hospital treatments and rehabilitation, long-term adjustment to life in a wheelchair and the return to his chosen career in medicine. His unique experiences give insight into medical recovery, life's challenges, human behaviour, the value of support and what he feels really matters in life. The doctor in the book is a patient, and so it is instantly appealing beyond the medical readership. The tables have been turned. It is about life at extremes. There are many interesting tales and lessons to be learned in this rare piece of narrative. The thrust of the book steers away from purely medical issues, which makes it all the more interesting and widely relevant. It is essential reading for anyone who wants to know more about life through this writer's unusual experience.

    It still seems almost unreal to me that he is me, that I am still alive, and that I have managed to write a book about it. It has been an incredible journey. I felt an obligation to write about my experiences simply because I have been so lucky to survive. Somehow I escaped death and here I am to tell the tale.

Chapter 1

16 March 1992: the unforgiving slippery slope of accidental change

I went on a skiing holiday in March 1992 to Val d'Isere in France with three friends. Two were from medical school, Andrew and Ellie, and the other person, Ian, was someone I knew through Andrew. After a long road journey to the resort from the airport, we managed to settle into our apartment and collect the necessary ski equipment for us to start skiing early the next morning. We had a self-catering apartment in a town called Le Villaret. It was about a mile or so from Val d'Isere town but, nonetheless, conveniently closer to the funicular than had we been in Val d'Isere itself. The funicular is the train that goes through the mountain and eventually drops off skiers at the summit.

On the first evening, we met Ellie's parents and more friends in Val d'Isere for supper. Hot food in cosy surroundings and with good company was a great way to start the holiday, as the chilly wind was heard outside. These others had been at the resort for a time already. In fact, two of them had been working nearby for quite some time. The holiday was just what we needed. I think all of us in our recently arrived party of four were very excited with the anticipation of skiing the following day.

We were all outdoor types. We enjoyed going up mountains. However, I must say that I was more cowardly than the others when it came to conquering mountains or "bagging peaks," as the enthusiasts or "mountain nutters" might say. Certainly, I didn't enjoy climbing. The other three were far more rock-face-friendly, having climbed Mont Blanc and some technically difficult climbs. I was too scared to do proper climbing. I valued my life sufficiently that I opted not to pursue a climbing pastime with zeal. People would argue that this is the inexperienced climber in me speaking and that scrambling is more dangerous than climbing with protection. I am not looking for an argument. I simply found that going up a vertical bit of rock tied on to ropes, in case I fell, as being rather unsettling on my psyche. It wasn't what I would call a good day out. I'm rather an ordinary bloke, with a fondness for self-preservation. This talk of my cowardice might sound rather out of character and paradoxical, in view of my having done a parachute jump and the like before. Whatever one's bravery, none of us can avoid doing anything with some danger and I don't think that it's healthy to go around worrying about doing anything adventurous in an almost paranoid manner. If we did, we would end up having a rather tedious and ordinary existence. And also, the parachute jump seemed to me to be a less protracted process than climbing. The treachery of climbing somehow seemed far more tangible, it could be very reliant on the weather and, once committed to going up a mountain, it was difficult to turn around. There was the potential of being stuck on a mountain and having to do something risky to get out of the situation. Fortunately, there was not going to be the threat of rock climbing on this holiday. It was just skiing, relaxation at bars halfway-down the slopes and apres-ski. How fantastic; I was here to have fun.

    The first morning was spent on the nursery slopes. After this short introduction, we were all ready to go to the mountain top for more challenging skiing. At the end of the day, there was that wonderful feeling when one feels fresh, clean and healthy, having enjoyed blue sky and crisp winds from a day's skiing on the pistes. The feeling is that of sensing an escape from the smog of the city to the beauty of the outdoor countryside. You feel refreshed and free from the shackles of urban life. I had been skiing once before on a week-long school trip, when I was sixteen. It's amazing how quickly skiing skills are regained. I was parallel turning and slaloming with confidence by the end of the day. It was incredible fun and I had only had a day's worth so far. We were all quite tired after a day's skiing and, having rested on our bunk beds, we headed on into Val d'Isere for food and drinks. I can remember being in a bar later that evening. Ellie was playing a board game with one of the locals. I briefly joined in. We hadn't overindulged in alcohol that evening. I guess that we were all a little shattered from our exertion that day. We were, nonetheless, intoxicated from the excitement of being on holiday.

    Next, we headed back to Le Villaret along the main road. The road was very slippery with an ice slush overcoat. The game on the road was to slide as far as you could. I recognised my limitations and likelihood of falling over, and so hung back doing half-hearted slides. We then arrived at the ski-slope which was near to our apartment. A small stream was nearby and a quick splashing of water at each other could not be resisted. After this, Andrew and Ian found some mats that they had seen people using on the ski-slope earlier that day. The mats were like large gymnasium mats, which you sat or lay on, to go down the slope. They indicated that we could take one of the mats a little way up the slope and have a go. Ellie said that she had had enough for the day and returned to the apartment. The three of us who remained dragged the mat up the slope a sufficient distance to have a go. Andrew lay on his front on the right of the mat, I did likewise on the left, and Ian sat on the back. I can remember going down the slope and having no control over where it went. This shouldn't have really mattered, since after all we were simply going down a designated ski-run and the mat should have come to an uneventful stop at the bottom. Unfortunately, it did matter. These mats go at a lightening-fast pace and it mat gathered speed mercilessly as it skimmed along the smooth snowy covering of the slope. Then it veered slightly to the left on the way down and the rest is history. I rely on what has been told to me for the details from here on.

  At the bottom of the ski-run, the mat went in the direction of a hut around which there was protection in the form of netting. This netting was similar to the crash barrier protection that you see on televised skiing events, such as shown on the BBC's Ski Sunday programme. It's the sort of protection that can dissipate a heavy impact, so that it is less damaging or even harmless. I can remember how I often viewed speeds of eighty miles-per-hour on television, as skiers clattered into these barriers. The skier would be a tangled mess in the fence protection. Then, they would stand up to dust themselves down and shake their heads clear of the collision. It was amazing how good this protection was. There is, however, a big "but" coming now for my case. Otherwise, I wouldn't be writing this book! BUT the protection around this hut had been vandalised in one area. Ian had fallen off the back of the mat and Andrew on the right side of the mat hit the intact protection around the hut. He was winded, but did not sustain any lasting traumatic injuries. I was unfortunate enough to impact where the protection had been vandalised. This meant that I hit the hut almost head-on. A lasting scar on my left cheek, my Zoro scar, indicates that I must have hit slightly more on my left side, rather than square-on with my head. Probably fortunate, as otherwise I might have sustained a more severe head injury and possibly a higher spinal cord injury, in other words a neck rather than back break, or perhaps even died.

 All the same, there was the stark reality of no going back on what had happened. The tragedy had now occurred. My life had been altered dramatically by this single episode of misfortune. It would never be the same again. I had many injuries as a result of the collision: fractured jaw on both sides, fractured left collar bone, about eight fractured ribs, broken back at midback level (T6 vertebral level, for the doctors) and injured spinal cord, pneumothorax on one side and a haemopneumothorax on the other side, lung contusions, and brain oedema and contusions. Contusion is the medical term for bruising as seen on a scan, and haemopneumothorax and pneumothorax are terms for a punctured lung. Unfortunately, as can be seen, I don't do things by halves. I was a mass of flesh and bones: broken flesh and broken bones. Andrew told Ian to run for help. Andrew remained with me. I was making splurting noises, but he didn't move me. I think that he tried to see if there was anything in my mouth obstructing my airway, causing me to make these noises. The rescue team was on the scene quickly. They put some pneumatic trousers on me, tested for response to different stimuli, put up drips to give me fluids and did anything else necessary to resuscitate me and keep me alive. I was transferred by road to the nearest hospital for further emergency treatment and my friends were left at the scene, not being allowed to come with me. What a nightmare for my poor friends. It was all right for me. I was unconscious and didn't have to, well at least couldn't, worry about anything.

 Shortly after my accident, the ski-resort people piled stacks of snow around the part of the hut that didn't have protection. At least now the same thing wouldn't happen to anyone else imminently, even though my own life had been significantly transformed already. It's just a few seconds to change your life forever. Is it fate? Am I lucky to be alive, despite having been unlucky to hit the hut? Whose fault is it? Is there anyone to blame? Is it better to get on with life, assuming these things to be destiny? And why have I been trying to justify my life before the accident as a particularly ordinary one? It's really to convey that this sort of thing could happen to anyone. What happened to me just came out of the blue, an unlucky hand for me on the day of the 16th March in 1992. I was simply a normal person. I don't believe that I was very different from most other people. I was not a progressive risk-taker, waiting for the accident to happen. I was enjoying my life and what lay ahead for me too much to do that. It was just bad luck: a tragedy. We all take risks of varying degrees in our daily lives. Bad luck can happen to anyone, whatever their background. Maybe my life was too good. Perhaps, before the accident, I thought that life couldn't be this kind, so much so that it couldn't stay like that for long. In retrospect, I try to imagine that I anticipated something bad happening; but then I reckon that that's my mind playing tricks on me. It's just speculation. I certainly didn't plan for or want the accident to happen. I think that my mind was mainly set on enjoying myself on the holiday, thinking that the risks of injury were low. My skiing hadn't been reckless. I was enjoying the skiing and I didn't need to take big risks to enjoy myself. It was going to stay that way for the rest of the holiday. The toboggan mat had been out of my control, though. Only afterwards can I appreciate the consequences of this one act, which appeared so insignificant until it all went wrong. I can't call out to that fit young man, show him what was going to happen, show him how his body was going to be broken, show him the struggle ahead for him and urge him not to get on to the mat. That youthful man is now a damaged person, both physically and mentally scarred. There's no going back to a former life, now lost.

  Should time be wasted trying to understand it, when there are no obvious answers? I feel that it is necessary to try to rationalise things in some way. You have to live with what has happened, and so somehow you have to get what has happened to you inside your head…..but you need to do this in your own time. You know that you have moved on from the torment of the accident, when you can truly say, "Let it be" and look to the future. All this I would have to do at a later time. Now was the time for fate and the medical resources and expertise around me to decide whether I would survive. Only if that went right, could this later rationalisation be attempted. What was apparent was that my life was in imminent danger: it lay precariously in the balance. My injuries were indeed life-threatening. If there had been any more, I probably would have died.

Chapter 2

Ghosts of a former life: my childhood

What was my background before this tragedy of 16 March 1992 befell me? Indeed is there anything special about me, other than nearly dying in my early-twenties, that privileges me to give insights into the human condition at such a young age? After all, I think of my background as not particularly out of the ordinary. I was born in 1970 in the city of Bristol, the youngest of four children. My childhood was a happy one, with my parents being ever supportive yet not overbearing. One of the many good things about my parents is that they don't appear to have any favourites among me and my siblings; and I don't think that this is the spoilt youngest child in me speaking. We were all treated fairly and we knew our limits of tolerable behaviour.

I enjoyed the usual things that youngsters do. I was fairly active with most sports. My hand-eye coordination was pretty good, and I used to be best at racket sports like tennis, squash, badminton and cricket. My running ability, mainly long distance, wasn't too bad either. Cycling used to be something done in my spare time and also I had to cycle a couple of miles to school each day. I enjoyed football and was less keen on rugby. My kicking ability far excelled my tackling ability. I was good, but never brilliant, at these activities. I was more of a slender swift person, rather than a powerful hulk. Golf became a hobby in my mid-teens and this is something that I became particularly good at, being in the top two or three at school. These were my main pastimes, so I was a physically active sort of bloke rather than a couch potato. I also played computer games and snooker. I was lucky enough to be given a small snooker table as my main present one Christmas. Many happy an hour were spent trying to get a high break at that table. Forty five was the best one, I think, so I was pretty average at it. As for things like reading, I wasn't very keen on that. It was only the threat of a school literary assignment that made me get down to reading books. So sporting activities, family and friends predominated in my childhood. I was pretty good at entertaining myself; I didn't get easily bored with my own company. I guess that my imagination could captivate me with very little effort.

My schooling was good and it offered me sound opportunities when it was time to embark on post-school life. I was fortunate enough to be able to go to medical school in London at the age of 18 and medical school was great fun. I made some very good friends and had some great times while I was there. It soon became apparent exactly how good they were, when I was involved in the accident of March 1992.

So why would I want to write about this tragedy? Why would I want to go over all the painful incidents? What good will come out of it all? Perhaps it's for my catharsis. Not really; this has mainly been achieved already. I guess that now I am more of an interesting person, or certainly my life story is more interesting, than when my life was going along swimmingly. When someone feels that he or she has important messages to tell, he or she should attempt to tell as many people as possible and a book can be a good way of achieving this.

The main messages to convey have been learned in my journey along the road of "life rehabilitation." I tend to be a non-confrontational person and try to find the least disturbing method to communicate a point to someone. I prefer discussions to arguments, answers to questions, and solutions to problems. I don't want to waste my opportunity of being able to communicate my messages to many people. I don't want this chance to slip right through my hands. I want my messages to get out to the World because I don't think that they only apply to people who have events that transform their lives dramatically. The messages could be applied to most people in everyday life. Everyone has scars from the past and life's challenges ahead. Everyone has been wounded by life in some way or another. It just so happens that some of my wounds are obvious external visible scars, such as a wheelchair and inability to walk. I also have lots that cannot be seen. Hidden scars and burdens are in all of us to some degree. Much lies behind the curtains of our exterior. Different people draw on different things for sources of strength. I know where mine have been found. The inspirational figures will become apparent.

Chapter 3

September 1988 to March 1992: medical school in London prior to the accident

I arrived at St Bartholomew's Hospital Medical School, London, in September 1988 to embark on my medical degree course, having almost exclusively lived in Bristol before this. This made it a major life event to be leaving the parental home for the first time. It was a fantastic college with just over 100 students in each year and I soon settled in. All us freshers were in the same boat. The lecture theatres were a couple of hundred yards from College Hall, the student accommodation block. The late-closing bar, where I had many good nights with my newly found mates, was on the ground floor of College Hall. This resulted in first year essentially centering around College Hall, which brought a welcome sense of community to the place. Also, College Hall was in central London, and so it was a great location for the novice to the London experience.

The first two years were preclinical, consisting of lectures, anatomy dissection sessions and some laboratory work. Examinations happened each term, the crucial ones being at the end of each year. The average week was fairly full. Memories of the first year are of two terms of late nights and rolling up to lectures feeling less than optimally focused, and a final term of cramming to get through the end of year exams. I earned the dubious nickname of "Tom the Vom" in Freshers' Week, when I was sick having overindulged in alcohol after football trials. Unfortunate because I have rarely been sick after alcohol, but the name stuck. The second year was slightly harder workwise and I was more consistent with my diligence. I did, however, manage to keep a passion for some extracurricular activities. I was a keen golfer with a handicap of six. I played for the London University team and was awarded university colours. The Alpine Club was also an enthusiasm. I very much enjoyed going on long walks or even scrambles to reach the summits of mountains. All inspired walkers will know how views are literally breathtaking from wonderful natural sights. I even managed to be persuaded to do the

Fourteen Peaks in 1991, with eight or so others. The task is to climb all fourteen mountains over 3000 feet high in North Wales in less than 24 hours. When I did this, there was very little time to sit down to admire nature's beauty. It was more a test of endurance. One needed to focus on the challenge ahead to get through it. It was an extreme test of stamina and mental character, but thankfully didn't involve climbing shear rock faces…….or is it "v. diff" that means shear, if you use the technical jargon? "I don't rightly know," I say in a rural accent to myself. And should I really care? In any case, quite a sense of achievement for me to have completed this feat, but I lost my two big toenails in the process. I suppose that there is often a price to pay for success. "You don't get something for nothing" and "no pain, no gain," is what some crazy aerobics fanatics enthusiastically recount to others. Sadly, there is sometimes a lot of truth in these sayings.

In my third year at college, I did an optional year of study at University College, London, to gain a BSc degree. This was a good year with a change of scenery from my medical school base. I was even cavalier enough to do a parachute jump on one occasion during that year. This didn't seem overly brave to me, though, because in the main all you have to do is jump out of the plane. The rest, such as opening the parachute, is usually done automatically for you. It is over before you know it, which luckily gives you very little time to worry about things. Quite an experience. In fact, it was absolutely brilliant. It wasn't so much the thrill of jumping out of the plane that was good. The special part was when the parachute was open and I drifted on the breeze. It was very calm, so much quieter than I imagined, as I descended to the ground. There was no rushing past of the wind. It was more as if I was suspended quietly in space. I guess that I was. All the same, it didn't give me the buzz to do it more than just the once. The only other thing that I could compare to this was when I went glider flying during this year. If you signed up with the University Gliding Club, you could go gliding at High Wycombe, about forty miles from London. I had done so and I travelled to the glider centre on my scooter, a 100cc Vespa, on four occasions. It was usually a pretty cold journey to get there, but well worth it. My four flights involved me in the front seat with my controls and an instructor in the seat behind me with his controls. We would be towed to about 2000 feet by a plane and release the tow-wire at this height. Then, we were on our own. It was a quiet peaceful feeling similar to the parachute experience to be floating without a motor sounding. I very much enjoyed it, but I didn't progress to being in the glider on my own. That would have been scary, as the lack of engine power made me feel that a mistake would be less forgiving than one made in a plane. The instructor had been my essential security during the flights. Nevertheless, all these activities were good fun and it was great to enjoy the fresh air.

    My first three years of college had long holidays and I certainly made the most of this. Admittedly, I had to do odd jobs to earn valuable cash during part of them, but I also managed to go on some good holidays. Inter-railing around Europe was done with two school friends after my first year. This was brilliant fun and we got as far as Greece with a fifty hour train journey through Yugoslavia. Our odour was less than optimal after being crammed up like battery-farmed chickens for this time. Still, we all stank and somehow that made it seem acceptable. It was definitely students doing it the rough way. We visited France, Italy, Yugoslavia and Greece in three and a half weeks. It was a good value holiday for so many things experienced and places visited. I was very much enjoying my youthful independence.

    After my second year, I went to Egypt and Israel for three weeks with two friends from college. One of the friends was half-Egyptian half-Yemeni and we stayed with his family in Cairo for the first week. It was good to see Egyptian life from someone's home. We even went to an Egyptian wedding. That was a truly mad experience. No alcohol and thankfully so because they were driving like maniacs as a celebration of the event. Our Egyptian Yemeni friend seemed to enjoy it when my other friend and I had to dance, the Egyptian way, in front of the whole wedding party at the request of the groom to much applause. It's amazing how generous people are with their praise, if you just enter into the spirit of things. It was understandably a truly happy atmosphere and all the people were very welcoming to us. After the first few days of meeting so many people, we went scuba diving in the Red Sea for five days. Further sightseeing in Southern Egypt followed this. Then two of us enjoyed a trip over to Jerusalem for a couple of days, with the Egyptian

Yemeni friend staying with his family in Cairo. It was a fantastic trip with many good memories.

As for my holiday after my third year, I travelled down the West Coast of France from Brittany as far as La Rochelle with John, a friend from childhood. Then we went along the Loire valley, through Le Mans along the racetrack of the car race staged a few days before, and back to Brittany. This holiday was done on a Lambretta 125cc scooter, with me as the driver and John the pillion passenger. It was a great adventure. Luckily, the scooter was reliable, even if not particularly fast. Top speed was about forty five miles-per-hour. It was a classic bike, having been produced in 1962. The leather seats for passenger and driver were separate, rather than the usual single padded seat, and the engine used to puff instead of purr. It was very much a hands-on bike, rather than one where the bike did all the work. It was a real joy to drive and travel on, even if the hard seats were a bit tough-going on the bum after a while. In one week, we travelled just over a thousand miles. We would normally set off at about nine-in-the-morning. After four or so hours on the road, we would reach our chosen destination for the day. Then, we would find a cheap hotel and shortly after that, we would often tuck into mussels, bread and wine. It was a great way to travel. As well as the freedom and independence of motorbike travel, it was really good to discover places by just bumping into them: preferably not literally. We felt like we were actually seeing France in a unique way, certainly different to a standard holiday. I very much valued these unconventional holidays. I can remember one evening going off on a short drive along the coastline, while John was resting at the hotel. The evening's warmth and calmness enabled me to go in short sleeves. As I drove, the breeze rustled past me, clear blue sky up above. I felt so liberated. I finally reached my desired viewpoint and got off the bike. I looked back on the coastal town. I thought to myself how wonderful life was, how lucky I was and how good it felt to appreciate it. All was well with the world.

Another brief break away was a motorbike ride to Paris to visit a school friend studying there. I was the driver again, with another school friend on the pillion. This was a slightly more hurried journey, in that there were no stops taken to admire a view or to discover a town. An Eastern block motorcycle, MZ 150, was the bike used this time. This was about twenty miles-per-hour quicker than the Lambretta. Even so, being November, it was a pretty tiring and cold journey. It had been an early start, setting off at four-in-the-morning. I think that it took about six hours on the road from London to Paris. The roads were fairly treacherous around Paris. I was as careful as possible, only too aware of the vulnerability of a motorbike. The trip was negotiated without incident, and we had a great time catching up with each other and having three days in Paris. I had a zest for adventure, while at the same time trying to minimise risks. I felt a responsibility even at this stage of my life, almost in a paranoid manner, not to endanger my fitness unnecessarily. It seems quite bizarre, in view of what was to happen to me on the fateful future skiing holiday. Whatever precautions are taken, there is a fine line between experiencing life and being safe.

After my year at University College, London, I returned to St Bart's in September 1991 to start the clinical part of the medical degree. This is mainly ward-based work and lasts three years, after which time you qualify as a doctor. There would be no more long holidays in the remainder of the course. During this time, you learn how to talk to patients, examine them, and to present your findings and thoughts on the case to a third person. Wards and, rather bizarrely, even patients are quite daunting when you start. I had done some holiday jobs such as nursing, operating theatre portering and cleaning floors in hospitals prior to this. Even so, I found the idea of going on the wards as a medical student quite nerve-wracking but, at the same time, exciting. I had almost done a year on the wards before my accident happened. By this time, I had developed a taste for and interest in hospital medicine, rather than purely lectures. Patients were interesting to talk to and examining them was a new skill that I was keen to perfect.... or at least to become vaguely competent at doing. Blood-taking, putting lines into patient's veins for fluid drips and helping in surgery were all refreshing things in which to be participating. I was in a privileged position; especially when I think how bad at blood-taking I initially was. Poor patients! Still, student doctors need to learn some way, and I feel that in many cases there is a reciprocal gratitude and obligation between medical staff and patients. My initial anxieties gradually lessened and in fact I was soon enjoying it very much.

My life ahead seemed to be an exciting prospect at that stage. I was training to be a doctor and felt that it was what I wanted to do. I had many hobbies, which I relished, and life was being enjoyed to the full, despite the financial limitations of being a student. My general fitness was very good, I got on well with all of my close family and I had some very good friends, both at college and back home. The main things that lay in front of me were my career and perhaps a family of my own. Life seemed very sweet, but I had not tasted much bitterness in my life's path up to this point.

Chapter 4

The first ten days: French hospital

My body and the illusion of life being easy had been shattered by the sudden impact with a solid wooden hut. Uncertainty and pain had now entered my life. I cannot remember anything about my time in France, from just before the accident and through my return to England by plane. This time must have been awful for my friends and family involved. These friends were present in France for the days that I was there and they were tireless in their efforts to get things done correctly. They tried to register the accident at the ski-resort, but were not allowed to do so and the reason for this remains a mystery that still perplexes me.

    My friends contacted my parents, Valerie and Peter, by telephone to inform them of the news and they came over to France with one of my brothers Alexander, also known as Ali, as soon as they heard the news. Obviously, they were stunned from hearing what had happened. This is the sort of situation that people dare not think about happening. I cannot know the feelings that they had. They have said how dreadful the situation was, but we have not talked about it in great detail. I don't think that any of us have felt the need. It's one of those unturned stones that we have not dealt with; but it doesn't necessarily need dealing with. What matters is that innately we know that it was purely devastating. Silence often speaks louder than words. When my parents arrived, I was unconscious, although my mother has said that she held my hand and had a response from me. I started to gain consciousness after two to three days. Initially, my wrists needed to be tied to the bed, so that I didn't pull at tubes and so forth. There were chest drains put in on both sides for my punctured lungs. I must have pulled out the drain on the left, as there are two chest drain scars on that side now.

    My condition was stabilised. On about day four after the accident, surgery to my jaw was performed. Wires were secured firmly in place on my teeth and jaw to fixate the fractures. A tracheostomy tube was inserted at the same operation. This is a tube, which goes through your neck directly into your windpipe, so that you can bypass your mouth to breathe. It's unclear whether this was inserted to prepare me for future ventilation that would be necessary during later surgery on my fractured spine or because of oral swelling from the jaw surgery potentially causing airway compromise. It was difficult for my parents and family to have as much involvement in my hospital care as they would have liked, since they couldn't speak the language very well. By that I mean French, and not just the language of medicine. Medicine can be double-dutch to the layman, but this was medicine communicated in French. Very confusing for my friends and family, and so they needed to place even more trust in the doctors than would be usual on home ground. Plating of the jaws is less obstructing to airway access than wiring them, and there is contention as to whether my fractured jaw should have been plated instead and no tracheostomy performed. In any case, wiring of my jaws and a tracheostomy is what was performed. What was done was done and this tracheostomy turned out to be a significant factor in my later hospital stay.

Chapter 5

Return to home ground

My condition remained stable over the next few days and it was decided to transfer me to England as soon as a suitable hospital could be found. A neurologist at Frenchay Hospital, Bristol, was a friend of my family and he was very helpful in arranging a bed for me in the hospital where he worked. Importantly, this was close to where my parents lived. As a result of negotiations, transfer to England happened about ten days after my accident. My family and friends were very relieved. They had been in a foreign country, unable to understand the language and hence all that was being done to me. At last they would have their home comforts, while they tended to my bedside in England. Other concerned family members and friends, who couldn't visit me due to the inconvenience of being in a different country, would now be able to do so. Family and friends manage to get through the stress of having to travel, if they can arrange it, but it was made more difficult by being injured in France. How selfish of me! You ask yourself why these things have to happen abroad; but, irrespective of where these things occur, what is the biggest nuisance is the fact that they have occurred at all. The unfairness of it all lies mainly in the fact that the injury has occurred, rather than the circumstances or place of injury.

  The day of my transfer by air ambulance from France to Bristol had come. My dad and brother had to make their own arrangements for returning home because there was only space for one family member on the plane. My mum had this honour, although I think that honour is a misleading way of phrasing it when you hear what it entailed. It was rather a dubious one and in fact terror might be a better word, but luckily she is a hardy lady. She was given some wire-cutters to carry during the flight and her role was to cut my jaw wires if I had problems with my tracheostomy and stopped breathing. I don't know why they couldn't have delegated this job to someone else, such as a paramedic. I guess that it was a crowded plane and they required all hands at work, if needs must. I also don't know why they would want the wires cut to get to my mouth, as my tracheostomy tube was a good airway through which to be ventilated. It almost seems like mentally torturing my mother: "Let's see how much this English woman can take! Give her these wire-cutters and tell her she has to ……." The French didn't really say that, before I get held up in court about it.

      The flight went uneventfully and the wire-cutters did not need to be called into action. My mother had gone grey haired at a young age and has it coloured regularly, and so on the bright side at least she didn't have to worry about the colour of her hair, resulting from this psychological torture. I was taken to Frenchay Hospital by ambulance from the airport. One of the wards there welcomed me back to the National Health Service and English speaking medical staff. What a weight lifted for my parents, back on home ground at last. They must have consequently felt slightly more in control now; but there was plenty more excitement and stress to come. I didn't do it deliberately,……honestly. I like winding people up, but the events that had happened and that were to happen were all a little bit beyond a joke. Also, it must be stated that I wasn't laughing.

Chapter 6

Frenchay Hospital: visitors, hallucinations, jaw plates, back rods, breathing difficulty and another moment to change my life forever

Frenchay Hospital is in South West England on the outskirts of the city of Bristol. It used to be an army barracks hospital and, as a result, is mainly on only one level. I had my back fixed here. By fixed, I mean that two metal bars, Harrington rods, were inserted in my back and attached to either side of my bony spine to support it at the fracture site. Also, a bone graft from my right hip was placed at the level of my back break to stabilise it further. Sadly, my spinal cord was not fixed. My spinal cord had been damaged and judged irreparably so at the operation. The spinal cord had not been snapped in half; it rarely is. It had been stretched and squashed, causing damage to it. This meant that I couldn't move or feel below the level of the lesion, which was that of the lower chest. At the same operation, my jaw was plated, the jaw wiring was removed and the tracheostomy was taken out of my neck.

All things seemed to be heading in the right direction, although there had been a period when neurosurgery was contemplated for my head injury. That would not have been a step in the right direction. I think that this was considered an option because of my brain swelling. After much watchful waiting, it was decided to leave my head alone and see if things would resolve naturally. My family can remember a poor outlook given on my brain recovery as a certainty by one of the doctors. Estimation of recovery is very difficult and recovery from this sort of injury can be a long process, with an open mind to the outcome being the best approach. I feel that one needs to take things day by day, rather than predicting too far ahead. Obviously, one should be realistic about things, but adopting an open-minded approach should enable most people affected to adjust to most eventualities and in their own time. Luckily, the predictions given turned out to be wrong. Phrasing with words like might, probably and possibly are far better than those of will, definitely and undoubtedly, when the doctor is communicating information on potential outcome in an uncertain situation such as was mine.

I was to spend three weeks here at Frenchay, having arrived at the end of March 1992. My main places of residence were the Intensive Care Unit and Ward 2, the ward housing predominantly neurosurgical patient cases. Visiting times and visitor numbers were limited and I have very disjointed memories of people during the time that I was there. I can remember different family members, friends, family friends, people from college and key nursing staff. The nursing staff were excellent, even though the whole situation was very disorientating. I was lying in bed for the whole time and I can remember trying to make sense of the different faces that would appear to me. It was confusing to me why so many people were interested in simply coming to say hello as initially I was doing little more than just lie in bed.

However, my breathing had progressively worsened since my operation and many tests, being done to look for the cause, were to no avail. My memories are of calling out for help and especially for a certain male nurse to reassure me when I couldn't get my breath. This nurse was doing a fantastic job at calming me down. It wasn't just panic, though, because the machine that displays the blood oxygen level was registering a lower than desired reading. I was getting bluer and more tired with each attempted breath. In fact, I was exhausted. How much longer could I go on, straining at getting air into my lungs? I seemed to be losing my battle for life, as all that friends and relatives could do was watch on. One evening, when I must have been close to death by asphyxia, my mum telephoned my dad distraught and in tears. She felt helpless and was desperate for something to be done, as I was fading in front of her eyes. Something dramatic had to be done to prevent my demise. My dad is a fairly eminent medical physicist and, fortunately, he knows some of the medical fraternity. He contacted the surgeon, who had done the surgery on my back, to discuss the situation. The surgeon had overheard the ward physiotherapist mention that my breathing difficulties could be related to where my tracheostomy tube had been.

Consequently, he got the ear, nose and throat surgeon involved to look into this possibility.

   I was taken to surgery and it was discovered that there was a narrowing of my windpipe, or trachea if you prefer medical terms, where the tracheostomy tube had been sited. It is known as a tracheal stenosis and this was an extremely tight one. The aperture of my windpipe was very small, only a couple of millimetres across at the scarred part: a pretty good reason for my breathing difficulty. Probably tracheal blockage rather than stenosis is more accurate wording. Another tracheostomy tube was inserted below the area of narrowing. This was for me to get air in and out of my lungs bypassing the obstruction, which was now present above the new tube. It had certainly been a life-saving procedure. Even though the new tube had relieved my breathing, a major consequence of the stenosis was that I couldn't project air up from my lungs past it and through my vocal cords to produce speech. I wouldn't be able to speak properly until this narrowing was corrected, but this was the last thing on my parents' minds. They were just glad to see me still alive. I had been very close to dying, yet again. This time must have been the most awful imaginable for them: to see their son dying before them, not being able to do anything. If my dad had not made enquires about my breathing, I **MAY** not be here. I stress may because I hate those sensationalised broadcasts of people's medical experiences, which are often one-sided, inaccurate and all blaming. It's unfair to point the finger irrationally and everyone was trying to do their best to help me. I simply want to demonstrate how close I came to death, rather than dwelling on the details of what happened.

   As I said, the events that occurred at Frenchay Hospital were very disorientating for me. I suppose that some people would say that I was "well out of it." There is one occurrence, which I do remember vividly because its clarity was in such a contrast to the hectic blur of events occurring. It must have been at the time when I was finding it very difficult to breathe. I was lying on the hospital bed and I can remember a voice very clearly saying this to me: "Do you want to carry on with all this fighting?; do you want to continue living?; do you want to go somewhere else?; do you want to go to another place?; it's such a struggle; is it worth continuing to fight it?; don't you just want to drift away?; it will be a peaceful and pleasant release from this battling"; and then the same voice continued: "or do you want to keep on living and be part of this world despite all this torment?; do you want to stay here?; do you want to remain in this place, to be in this world?; are there still things that you want to do?" I remember it so clearly. The voice was like a thinking voice; it was as if my thoughts had been voiced, although the voice came to me with me unaware that I had consciously had a thought. "Do you want to go? Do you want to leave this place?" There was a familiarity and a calmness giving me a choice of "leaving this place" and continuing a journey elsewhere rather than being asked "Do you want to die?" and that being the end of it. I had power in that it felt that whatever I chose to happen would happen. I don't know from where the voice came. It certainly wasn't someone by my bed because it was as if I had been removed from the chaotic environment of the ward. All of a sudden, I was at peace with myself. There had been so much commotion, so much struggle. But, for this moment I was in my own little shell.

    This moment had so much clarity and quietness, especially in comparison to the disrupting atmosphere of everything that had been happening before. It was unforgettable because of my apparent release for a few minutes from the turmoil that had been present. I felt safe with whatever choice I made. Neither dying nor fighting to stay alive seemed daunting. I was somehow free. I was free to choose my fate, although staying alive did also depend on the cause of my breathing difficulty being discovered. It was an amazing feeling to be about to die and yet feel so undistressed about it. The place where I was going was truly beautiful. I've never experienced anything like it before or since. Nevertheless, I wanted to stay alive. I didn't feel ready yet to give up life and go to this place. It was like me being given an offer of life, to continue life, to have a second chance at having a life. It was clear to me that I wanted to carry on living. It was clear to me that I still had a great deal to fulfil in my life. In many ways, life was so much clearer now: from this moment on, every day for the rest of my life would be a bonus. It was almost as if someone else was inside my head asking the questions and I replied to this, "Yes, I want to live still. I want to be able to do more with my life. I want to experience more life. There is still so much more for me to do. I can achieve so much more with my time, if given a chance. It will almost be a waste of life."

I honestly believe that I would have died, if I had answered that I did not want to live. At that moment, I had made a subconscious decision to continue fighting against whatever was happening to me. Since working as a doctor, I have seen many people die in hospital and how it appears that sometimes people can choose when they want to die. I think that I have actually been at my own personal crossroads where that decision is made. Strangely, it almost feels as if I have died because I think that the feeling of peace, which I had at that moment, is how it feels when near death. It was an amazing experience, probably the most significant one of my life. I don't consider myself a hero for surviving. I was purely lucky. Had I not had the medical input and the problem remained undiagnosed, I would not have pulled through, however much I wanted to survive. There is a lot of chance to the outcome of these situations. The fact that I said to myself that I wanted to live simply gave me a chance to live; but only if everything else went right. If I had wanted to die, though, I would have certainly done so. The decision didn't cure me, but it did give me a little longer to fight against death as being the outcome. It was an experience to alter my life forever, both physically and spiritually.

The feelings that I had when close to death are difficult to recapture, despite the experience leaving me with a lasting and unperturbing familiarity of my own mortality. I wouldn't like to rediscover the breathlessness, but the feeling of peace and detachment when on borrowed time was wonderful. Music can be very soothing and a song, "Flown Away" by Lene Marlin, manages to get me near to that feeling of peace, both through its words and melody. Years on, it reminds me that life need not always be a rush and that I should occasionally take time out from the pressures of the present, as I did when I almost died. Being able to have a reminder like that is really powerful in that it helps me get perspective. I can see how far I have come and that living and enjoying life in a full way is what matters.

It has been asked whether it is worth people visiting someone in hospital, when the person is dreadfully ill. I didn't interact with every visitor, but I knew that there were lots of people concerned for my welfare. There would always be a friendly face or hand for comfort. I felt wanted in this world. This must have had some effect on my decision to try to keep living…..experience more life….continue valued and loving relationships. It was a life-defining moment. Thank you to you all. Consequently, now I take each day as it comes with gratitude; each day is a bonus. My life has a new perspective that is not just linked with being in a wheelchair. Having been so close to death has greatly strengthened me as a person. I very much value this hidden perspective of mine. Very few people are lucky enough to have it. It is truly liberating to have been so close to death because somehow it makes me appreciate life for what it gives me rather than worrying about what I might be missing. Now I have to get on with living, share my experiences with others when appropriate and give a little back to all those who were there for me. It's the least that I can do. It is almost a duty to make the most of what opportunities I have been given.

    I can remember different faces surrounding my bed, when people were allowed to visit. I was often too ill to interact. I can recollect one occasion, when a really good friend came to see me for the first time. I have known him for most of my life, and so by inference we went back a long way. I sensed that I was very ill and not a sight to behold. This friend came on to the ward with a couple of others. He approached the bed and then had to turn around to walk out of the ward without a "hello." We did catch each other's gaze, though. His shocked expression was all that I saw. He came back on the ward a few minutes later. He had clearly been upset by what he had seen. It was apparent to me that I was truly in a desperate situation. He must have found it difficult for some reason. Was it my transformed state from when he had seen me a few weeks before my accident, the difficulty that I was having with breathing at the time of his visiting or the fact that I looked as if I was dying? I have never asked him about it. It was obviously a very distressing time for everyone involved. What was life doing to me? How did I end up in this situation, when a short time ago life was so comparatively uncomplicated? I was never going to be the same again. But, was I going to see much more life in any case? It could easily have been my time to die. Somehow I survived.

    Hallucinations were a problem while at Frenchay Hospital. Narcotic drugs had been used for pain relief and hallucinations can be a side effect. For me, there were three in particular. One was the appearance of tarantula spiders coming out from light-fittings in the ceiling and cracks between the ceiling tiles. They would run all over my bed. I can remember my dad having to pretend to stamp on them and flick them off my bed. My friend Andrew had bought a tarantula, when I shared a flat with him and three others in London and the spider used to be housed in a glass cage. Even so, I am sure that, in view of my narcotic-induced visions, Andrew might have doubted his wisdom of previous spider purchase. Another hallucination was that of snakes coming down my oxygen tubing; fortunately, this is not vivid in my memory. And, no, Andrew had not bought a snake when I lived in London. There's only so much a West Country boy like myself can take. The other hallucination, very memorable to my parents, was when they entered my hospital room once. I screamed to them that I had been surrounded by Zulus and that I had dealt with all but one of them. There was a poor black-skinned nurse cowering in the corner of the room. She left the room fairly rapidly, to my embarrassed parents' apologetic muttering. Let's call it surrender. I think that my parents must have wondered what I would do next.

  These following bits I don't remember. My mum told me about a conversation that I had with a friend called Gavin from Bristol, while lying in bed at Frenchay. I said, "Come on, Gav. Go and get the ski equipment from our room. We're going out skiing." He said that he didn't have any skis. In fact, he had never been skiing. He mouthed this to my mum, as I continued, "Yes, you have. They're in our room on the second floor of the apartment block. Go and get them." Very bizarre behaviour. Then there was another time, when both my brothers visited. They stood by my bed and, apparently, I told them to do something useful rather than standing there like two idle pink flamingos. There were many other people who visited. I dread to think what else I said. I guess that developing a windpipe narrowing to make me mute prevented me saying the wrong things. I think that that's looking a bit too much on the bright side of bad luck, though.

  My weight had plummeted due to all these stresses. I had gone from just below twelve stone before the accident to just over seven stone. My body had the image of a concentration camp victim. The decision was what to do next. Should I have my tracheal stenosis repaired or should I go to a Spinal Injuries Unit for rehabilitation? The ear, nose and throat surgeon in Bristol was keen to operate. He wanted to cut out the scarred section of windpipe and rejoin the remaining ends together. This might have necessitated detaching my lungs from their anchors, so that they could be raised sufficiently to join the two ends of windpipe together. It sounded like high risk surgery and I wasn't in the best physical condition for it. I was unable to discuss this to make an informed decision and it was down to my friends and family to act as my advocates.

    Friends in London enquired about what operations were available for my tracheal stenosis and who was the appropriate surgeon. It turned out that the surgery was not a straightforward undertaking. There were several operations of differing complexities available. A surgeon from the Royal National Throat Nose and Ear Hospital, Gray's Inn Road, London, could perform a different operation to the one already offered. This operation was more sophisticated and a less invasive one than the other one mentioned. It certainly didn't involve the threat of lung elevation. Also, my transfer to the Spinal Injuries Unit (SIU) in Salisbury had been agreed and the consultant there said that I should come down for strengthening up and rehabilitation before even considering surgery. This was sound advice. I was in no fit state for major surgery and, in this compromised state of health, healing of surgical wounds would not be optimal. I had also developed a pressure sore on the skin at the bottom of my back, in my buttock cleft, during my stay at Frenchay Hospital. I needed expert nursing in a specialised centre to get over this. The London throat surgeon also preferred to wait for a few months to see if the tracheal stenosis improved on its own, which would make surgery unnecessary. Surgery was not to be undertaken lightly. It was a difficult technical procedure and I think that he was the only surgeon in the country to offer the type of operation planned. He was going to visit me in Salisbury in due course.

    So it was off first to the Spinal Injuries Unit, as opposed to having further immediate surgery in Bristol. The Spinal Injuries Unit is officially called the Duke of Cornwall Spinal Injuries Unit, but located in Odstock, near Salisbury, rather than somewhere like Truro or Mevagissey as the name suggests. It was a wise choice to get me to Odstock Spinal Injuries Unit and to attempt surgery at a later date. I had had enough complications along the hospital path already. It hadn't been an obvious choice, though. My parents, family and friends had done lots of thinking and talking with many different people, with not always the same advice, before they had made this decision. They had done all the necessary investigating to make an informed choice. Thank goodness they were intelligent, calm and objective enough to make a sensible one for me. Thank goodness they had the connections to make the relevant enquiries. Many people in my situation would not have the benefit of such involvement by family members and friends.

Chapter 7

Odstock: the journey down

It was the end of April 1992 when I was to be transferred to Odstock Spinal Injuries Unit by road ambulance. I had to lie down on a stretcher for the journey. My dad, a nurse from Ward 2 at Frenchay Hospital and the two ambulance men were the occupants in the transporting ambulance with me. It was quite a bumpy journey. My dad did his usual utmost to make the journey pass with jollity. He would give a running commentary of what was going on out of the window. It lasted about two and a half hours in total. I can remember the yellow elephant being described outside the Happy Eater, one of my dad's favourite eating locations just behind the Little Chef chain of restaurants on his snack stop top ten. My dad is thankfully good at talking about life and making amusing conversation based on observations. He often needs no response to prompt him. This is just as well, what with me being mute due to my throat problem and the ambulance men were not much better. My dad and the nurse were my entertainment for the journey. They did well, as I remember the humour and laughing more than the bumps on the journey.

    Odstock is in a lovely part of the country. There had been a toss up between Rockwood SIU in South Wales and Odstock SIU. I think that I was fortunate to end up somewhere like Odstock. Beautiful scenery, on which to gaze out, can help a lot when you are trying to ponder the meaning of life and your situation. The hospital is set a mile or so out of Salisbury. The main view is rolling green fields and meadows: just what the doctor ordered.

Chapter 8

Odstock: arrival, impressions and initial progress

I can remember arriving at Odstock and being greeted by my sister Lucy, my mum and the person who was to be my primary nurse. I was wheeled on the stretcher to the ward. It's a rather strange view from lying flat on a stretcher. I watched lots of interested faces peer down on me. It was like how I would imagine it to be a baby in a pram or cot. At least no one uttered, "cuchi-coo" or "eh-oh." Certainly no one said, "Oh, isn't he cute? Such a pretty little thing." More likely to be said would be, "Cor! What a scrawny git. Get a haircut!" My ward was to be Avon, the other being Tamar. I was destined, as a new recruit, to be placed in the eight-bedded part of the ward. This is where people are put early on after injury.

It is always daunting when you change location. I was not particularly worried, though. After all, I had almost died already. What could be more frightening than that? My family visited almost every day that I was at this hospital. This is quite astonishing in view of it being sixty miles each way from where they live. Various staff members made me welcome. Kathy was to be my physiotherapist. The physios push you to become fit, among other things, and this isn't an easy job when their clients have been in bed for a few weeks. While you're in bed, your designated physio does passive stretching of your legs to limit contractures developing, gives you breathing exercises to do, and also gets you to do weight-work with sand bags or weights to increase your upper body strength. Being taught how to turn yourself over in bed is another task of the physio. When the patient has advanced sufficiently to be allowed out of bed, the physio also teaches balance and wheelchair skills, and how to transfer from wheelchair to bed, chair, car or floor. A floor transfer should ideally not be falling out of your chair. It should really be a controlled lowering, which is not always the case. I was a long way off transfers at this stage, I must say.

Thankfully, Kathy turned out to be a good laugh and easy to get on with. She was also good at her job. I felt that her humour helped with the rehabilitation process, rather than make it stagnate. We would chat about anything and nothing in particular, despite my capability to communicate being quite limited because of my lack of voice. It made me feel like Tom, rather than a patient, when I definitely needed to hang on to who I was. It also broke the monotony and often frustration of trying again and again and again to learn new tasks. Again and again and again isn't a typing error; the practising of tasks did literally happen over and over and over until I was sick of them. Practice was essential. It didn't make perfect, but close enough to it. These skills were needed for me to live as independently as possible. I would be able to focus on rehab during my physiotherapy sessions, but at the same time look at what I might want to do when I left the hospital and think about my interests. It's very easy to become institutionalised otherwise.

I had the privilege of having two primary nurses. Most patients only have one, so goodness knows why I had two. The primary nurse's role is to educate you about spinal cord injury and give you tips on how to manage your condition on a daily basis. Then there is the occupational therapist. Lisa was mine. OTs, as they are called, assess you for how you manage daily functional activities, such as making tea, washing, dressing, reading, writing and so on. They come up with devices and equipment to help you function better. This can be in the guise of home adaptations, wheelchair, car adaptations and so forth. Their input overlaps with that of a physiotherapist in a few areas. A social worker is delegated to each patient, too. Paul was my social worker and he helped sort out benefit payments and housing issues, as necessary.

The ward nurses are integral to success at rehabilitation. They are highly experienced in nursing spinally-injured people and also very supportive. The ward sisters and charge nurses have responsibility for the nurses, as well as helping out on the ward. They are a varied breed. Sister Win, strict but good fun; Sister Elizabeth, dare to call her Liz at your peril; and the ward Charge Nurse, well-meaning but unknowingly annoyed me at times, although being annoyed could easily be me being stir crazy without knowing it. Certainly, when you're in a closed environment for long enough, you pick up on most aspects of different people's behaviour. In retrospect, no one was actively unhelpful and most were excellent. Everyone had some fault, if you looked hard enough. I probably did a lot of looking as well, by being in hospital for such a long time and needing to entertain my mind in some way. A bit of frustration from the situation in which I found myself might have meant that I was more critical than usual. Even so, I don't think that I am much more critical than other people are. Ask my friends, but not my enemies please. I'm sure that there are lots of my habits that could be made public and certainly not to my advantage. That's why it's good that my enemies, if indeed I have any, aren't writing the book. Out of courtesy, though, I will try to keep unnecessary bitchiness to a minimum.

So it was the eight-bedded section of the ward where my Odstock career started. I stared at the same bit of ceiling for six weeks. I would play different games with lines on the ceiling, try to spot a new feature or bit of dirt, and just think about anything. My ceiling concentration would be interrupted every few hours by regular turns on to either side of my body, performed by the nurses, for skin pressure relief. The turn is more technically known as a "log roll" in which I guess that I am the log being rolled carefully to one side by two or three nurses. This is so that during the process there is not too much twisting of my body, in particular my back. A pillow is then placed between the knees and one behind the back longways for support. When you can't move or feel the lower part of your body, your skin marks if pressure is maintained on the same area for too long. All these measures helped minimise the chance of this happening. In addition to this, bed baths and general continence needs had to be addressed. Such was my routine as a patient confined to bed. The nurses saw to this initially. All these care measures, though essential, result in disturbed sleep, but this didn't greatly matter, as I was in bed all day at the beginning in any case.

As you progress in your rehabilitation at the Spinal Injuries Unit, you are advanced down the ward to gradually smaller ward areas until you are in a single room. I was a long way off being in one of the few single rooms. As well as ceiling gazing, I enjoyed having a television at my bed space. Luckily, I am amused easily by the majority of television junk-viewing…….Oprah Winfrey, Saved by the Bell, Ricki Lake….what trash, but mindless relief. I had better stop this list, rather than give free advertising to this rubbish, even though it's not all praise. The sound of music was also a pleasure to have. That's not "doe a deer a female deer" Sound of Music, but the ability to listen to music. It was a huge strength…..echoes in my brain of past memories to pull me through struggles. I wasn't really interested in doing anything too mind-stretching at this early stage. My brain needed its own pace to adjust to what had happened. I enjoyed being able to think, to escape in my head. I didn't feel that I needed much mental stimulation at all. Familiar faces, refeeding and time to think were my necessary ingredients for repair at this stage.

    My physio would visit me about once or twice a day at this stage to give me leg stretches and general encouragement. In my current state of being mute and bed-bound, we couldn't build up a very good working relationship. There was also not such a need for therapist input as there would be later on. My occupational therapist had a little input at this stage, providing gadgets to see if my time in bed could be made more interesting. A reading frame was tried. This was a device which could have a book attached and held above me, so that I could read it without my or other people's arms getting tired. It sounds like I'm a lazy young sod, but in all honesty I was so weak at this time that holding a book to read simply exhausted me. I just wanted to rest, be refed and somehow regain my stamina of a former life. I didn't crave for anything. If I had done, I would have gone mad. I adapted to the situation in which I found myself. Anything like a bath or a good film to watch was purely a luxury, not a necessity. It was great to have so many people visiting. This was, however, at times very tiring; but visitors were sacrificing a lot of their time and effort to come, so they deserved at least a reciprocal effort on my part. The long road of rehabilitation was going to teach me much about how regaining stamina and reaching goals is not easy. The time and struggle to regain one's stamina is much more than that involved in losing it.

    One other need was that of a general cleanliness. My hideously long hair was probably better phrased as big hair. I had had bed baths with flannels and water bowl for weeks, but had had no chance of a proper wash in a bath or shower. There was a contraption called a shower trolley. A patient could be kept flat and slid across on a special blanket from their bed to the shower trolley. My time had at last come for the shower trolley experience. It is always a bit nerve-jangling, when you are moved into a new device from somewhere that you have grown accustomed to and had many things done for you; in other words, the apparent security of my bed. These anxieties were unfounded, although I had to be careful not to let too much water from the showerhead go down my tracheostomy tube and drown me. It was like paradise having a proper wash and my hair, even though still big, was at last clean; no more dreadful itching. Each time a new breakthrough came, and showering in the trolley felt like a breakthrough, I would feel more normal, more human. The treat of the shower trolley was only one to two times per week, as it was naturally a device in demand, especially for tetraplegics early on in their rehabilitation.

After several weeks at the Spinal Injuries Unit, it became apparent that the brain injury sustained at the accident did not have any permanent consequences. Even so, there wasn't a great deal of things for me to do other than smile at visitors (I couldn't speak after all!), have the occasional passive leg stretch, flex the occasional active biceps fibre (small as they were at this time), eat and sleep. I had lost so much weight that I needed a tube down my nose into my stomach to feed me, so-called nasogastric feeding, in addition to consuming hospital food and high calorie milk shakes. The palatability of these drinks was very dependent on flavour and the mood that I was in at the time. The hospital food was surprisingly good. At a later date, when more aware of the options not on the regular menu, I realised that treats like cheese and ham toasties, bacon, egg and chips were available on special request. Well, actually special request meant simply writing these items on the bit of paper with the menu choices, rather than ticking against the choices offered. This made the hospital cuisine even better. It was one of the biggest advantages of becoming more with-it, as you progress in the direction of recovery. When you're stuck in an institution for a long time, food is highly valued. My mum used to bring in sandwiches for me. Avocado and bacon were my favourite, lovingly prepared by my mum's caring hands. Chopped bits of crispy bacon were interspersed amongst juicy avocado, the delicious mixture being placed between two pieces of fresh bread. What a saliva-stimulating delight. I would often anticipate a treat at lunchtime, if my mum had said that she would be visiting. The way to an impaired institutionalised man's heart is especially through his stomach.

I was provided with weights of one or two kilograms while on bed-rest. I was supposed to use these to prepare me for the physiotherapy that lay ahead, but it was difficult to get full motivation at this stage. After a period of time in bed, with regular turns to help my sacral skin-sore heal, it was time to get me out of bed. This was not as straightforward as it sounds. There was a risk of me fainting on sitting upright, having been horizontal for so many weeks. Also, being paralysed doesn't do many favours for sustaining blood pressure and preventing dizzy spells from not enough blood going to the head.

A tilt table, as it is known, was the first bit of equipment to adjust me to a more vertical perspective of the world. The patient is attached to a padded rectangular body-length slab in the supine position by straps that are secured to the upper and lower body. This is so that, when the slab is made more vertical, the paralysed individual stays attached to it rather than being flung forward to the ground. The usual routine for me, and I'm sure for some others, was: tilt, dizzy-head-spin, down, then tilt a little more than before, spin, down. I felt rather like a laboratory animal strapped to a board and being experimented on each day. Usually, my physiotherapist and occupational therapist would be the experimenters. Experimenters is not directed in a critical way, as the ordeal wasn't done without a bit of humour. It did, nonetheless, almost feel like a school practical experiment at times. It was a means to an end, though, not always apparent to me at the time. These experiments did eventually bear fruit, in that I was soon able to sit in a wheelchair. I enjoyed the tilt table, too. No, I'm not a nutter that likes getting dizzy. What I liked was a vertical view of my surroundings, something that can do the psyche a lot of good after having been flat for so long. It made it possible to interact with people on a more equal level. It was a step forward with rehabilitation. I will have to be careful not to sicken people with these double meanings…..step forward, jump forward, lucky break. Shall I go on? I ask you, who's kidding who about stepping? Despite the sessions on the tilt table, moving from it to being in a wheelchair was still a big step. I can remember quite often having to be tilted back in my wheelchair, on becoming dizzy.

To make matters worse, soon after getting out of bed into the wheelchair for the first time, I developed a dreadful headache. It was the worst headache that I've ever had. It was horrendous, so bad that I'm sure pain-killers would have not even touched it. It felt like my head was going to explode. I was also sweating profusely above the level of my injury. I let one the nurses know. They hurriedly lifted me with the help of others back into bed. I had had my urinary catheter removed earlier that day. In its place, I was wearing a urosheath connected to a leg-bag for collecting urine emptying from my bladder. The urosheath is an adhesive condom device with an opening at the end to attach to the leg-bag. Having been assessed by one of the nurses, it was thought that my bladder was not emptying. The urosheath was removed and a catheter was put back in my bladder instead. Just over a litre of urine was drained. Usually the maximum bladder capacity is about 400 millilitres, so my bladder was filled to almost three times its normal capacity. My headache resolved and it was such a relief. I thought that I was going to die, it felt that bad.

I had developed something called autonomic dysreflexia. This is a condition that can affect anyone with a spinal cord injury above a certain level. It happens because the sympathetic nervous system is affected, and any irritant stimulus below the level of spinal cord injury can cause increased sympathetic nervous activity above the level of injury. This results in sweating, skin changes, headaches, high blood pressure and so forth. It can be life-threatening, if not recognised promptly. The action to be taken, if these symptoms are encountered, is to look for a cause of the problem and to correct it. In this case, it had been an overfull bladder. Another thing to do is to take a pill called nifedipine, which should hopefully lower dangerously elevated blood pressure. My mum affectionately calls these my suicide pills. Autonomic dysreflexia might be yet another issue to contend with, although in all fairness it has never happened again as badly as this memorable occurrence. This spinal cord injury thing seemed to keep bringing me surprises.

I can remember how my imagination used to run vividly during these times of bed-rest. You would probably think that you would get dreadfully bored just staring at a wall or ceiling for a couple of months. I didn't get bored. There was no getting away from my physical predicament but I could escape in my mind, in my ceiling gazing, in my dreams. I was in Tom's imaginary world where anything could happen. It's quite an opportunity that is not usually possible at that stage in my life. I could simply lie in bed for a long time, thinking about anything and everything, without people calling me a lazy slob. "Look at the good in everything, mate, and you'll not be a miserable young git." Images would go through my head, as I fought the situation I was in. I can remember thinking of a film that I had seen on a couple of occasions. It's called Marathon Man starring Dustin Hoffman and Lawrence Olivier. Dustin Hoffman was a keen runner preparing for a marathon, believe it or not! It's all in the title, I'm told reliably. Jokes aside, Hoffman would imagine a black long distance athlete, when he needed to push himself just that little bit further for success in testing situations. I saw the same black athlete, as I lay in bed, in a way to succeed and survive my trauma. When I felt things were tough, this athlete would appear. He was continuing his running and me continuing my fighting. I would just see a profile of the black athlete's face focusing on the road ahead. The head would bob backwards and forwards, as further distance was covered. There was concentration in the athlete's face and nothing was going to overcome it to break him. The finish was never visible. All that was needed was concentration. I did not need sight of the finish. I did not know where my finish line was. I still don't years after my accident, if I'm honest with myself; but I'm in more control now. No one is ever in full control of their life's path. It's just that some people just think that they are and they're probably the ones who fall harder, when things do go wrong. The recovery from major trauma is a marathon; and you need a good team for success. It's not a solo effort, as all good athletes will tell you. So should I be thanking Hoffman? No, but the old silver screen can be inspirational when you might not expect it to be.

  I was pale, extremely thin, had really long hair and I couldn't speak. I found out later that some of the ward staff thought that I looked like the film character Edward Scissor Hands. Quite weird in other words. Some of the nurses have told me that they didn't know how to make me out, when I first arrived at Odstock. Not everyone knew exactly why I couldn't talk. Some thought that it was probably that I was shy, others that I was quite insular as a result of my accident and it was my way of coping, and a few were simply down right scared of me, the silent psychopath. It's difficult to know how I would have been had I had a voice. I am not the most vociferous person but, certainly, not having my windpipe complication would have led to less time in hospital and less frustration. It was, however, truly an enlightening experience.

My bed-space was surrounded by cards, draped over strings attached up high. I would frequently gaze at these wondering who had sent them, who knew about my situation and what effect this had had on these people. Was I known as the idiot that got injured, one of life's tragedies or just not thought about? The fact that there were so many cards - literally hundreds - made me feel that people were with me, people really cared. Lots of people had taken the time to think about me and my family. I was very lucky to have such friendship and support. People can give so much by just letting you know that they are there for you in spirit, if not physically. What must be stressed, however, is that so many did attend physically: quite unbelievably uplifting. I am not a tearful person, but emotions inside me stir when I recollect all that was done. If some people didn't visit at all or as frequently as they would have liked to, I could fully appreciate that it could have been awkward logistically or even upsetting seeing me. Whatever the reason, I didn't and don't hold it against anyone. I was just pleased to see whoever would come; and, after all, I was hardly the most entertaining person to visit, being mute and immobile.

Sometimes you don't need words to sum up what has happened. I can remember reading a card sent to me by a fellow student who had written, "What bad news. What can I say?" These sentiments reinforced how I was feeling: dreadful things do indeed happen, but it is impossible and futile to try to talk about what has happened to make it better. Words don't get rid of the problem, even though talking to the right people at an opportune time can be helpful for adjustment to your new situation. It is very difficult to find the right words. Those who experience the tragedy with you realise that it is all more than words. All you can do is simply acknowledge the tragedy and try to get on with the present and future. There was another memorable card that made me chuckle and it reminded not to lose humour at these times of trouble. It read on the front, "No more grapes please," and then the inside message was, "Bring money instead!"

Chapter 9

Odstock: further progress

You get to know the other patients well when you are in a hospital together for long time periods. The different broad categories are: walkers, being the ones whose spinal cords are sufficiently undamaged such that they can still walk and often have control of their bladder and bowels; paras, not paratroopers I jest perversely, but those who have broken backs and require to use a wheelchair because they cannot walk; tetras, which sounds like aliens from some space sci-fi television series or perhaps even a computer game, but they are in fact those people with broken necks and who often require a motorised wheelchair because of both leg and arm weakness. Virtually everyone who is admitted to the Spinal Injuries Unit has a tragic story of bad luck; by definition, being in the wrong place at the wrong time. It would be easy to feel sorry for yourself, but you are surrounded by those with equally bad or worse scenarios. It makes you realise that life is often unfair. You can see that life's unfairness is directed at lots of people indiscriminately, not at just you. It is also difficult at this early stage to take in all that has happened, whether this be due to denial, confusion, a self-protection mechanism or whatever else.

Who were the memorable patients? And with whom do I still keep in contact? There are many memorable patients. I learned so much by being with people with a similar impairment and at different stages of rehabilitation. It is good to see that you are not alone. It is also valuable to see what people can achieve. Sometimes you can't imagine ever being able to do certain things. Then, five years have suddenly passed and you're doing far more than the target that you set yourself. You are doing things that you didn't even consider possible. It's quite bizarre. You can only say that you can't do it, until you have tried it many times and failed. I have learned to be open with my capabilities and prepared to surprise myself and others. One should not set rigid limits on what can be achieved. We all set ourselves different goals to aim for and need to have hope for the future.

Having rigid limits imposed tends to be unproductive and can lead to the person becoming disillusioned. Someone's hope needs to be dealt with carefully and not unthinkingly dismissed. Limits to what can be achieved should be decided by the affected individual and only when that person has been given the necessary opportunities. It is a process of trial and error. One needs to focus on capabilities, not on deficits. The biggest fool is the closed-minded blinkered individual. Such an individual is usually someone who has had no experience of the recovery process; in other words, Joe Bloggs, who has had no exposure to what living with an impairment actually entails. Joe Bloggs here could equally be a doctor or a member of the public. It's life experience which matters more than medical training. Having a shallow attitude is the worst and probably the saddest disability. The difficulty is that those who have it rarely recognise it.

    When I was able to sit in a wheelchair without fainting, it was time to build up how long I could stay in the chair during the day. I was horrendously weak and it was very tiring, especially when all that I had been used to for the previous few months was lying in bed. It was also necessary to wear a body brace when sat in the wheelchair. This was a plastic contraption, which was buckled tight around the chest and torso area to stabilise my spine and allow sitting upright. The body brace needed to be worn for the first few weeks of mobilisation and it was really uncomfortable. It would add to what I initially considered as torture in the chair. It was difficult to know whether all the pain was due to the brace or to the damage that had been inflicted on my body. I felt like a broken toy. "Can't I just buy a new one rather than go through all this turmoil?" I would sometimes think to myself in desperation of my situation.

    I can remember getting extremely weary after a very short time in the wheelchair. At this stage, I couldn't lift my bum off the seat using my arms in a push-up technique on the wheels, and so a special inflatable Roho cushion was supplied. This type of cushion would relieve pressure from my buttock area and prevent skin marking, which could have happened with a standard foam cushion. The downside of the inflatable cushion was its unsteadiness making it very difficult to balance on. It was like being on air, plus I couldn't feel my bum. The ability to progress on to a foam cushion would at least improve unsteadiness. Bum sensation is a rather more difficult thing to rectify. Prayers or major scientific advances spring to mind. I wonder which might work first!

I was reliant on the nurses to lift me back into bed because I couldn't lift myself across at this stage. It was a real test of endurance, mental and physical, to wait to be lifted. When I had been able to sit in the chair for more than a couple of hours, it was time to go to physiotherapy to start weight-work. Physiotherapy was about 150 yards down the corridor. Pushing the wheelchair, a heavy old NHS one I stress, was extremely tiring and limited to a few yards. Balance was also precarious. It would be bad enough as an able-bodied person in a wheelchair. My inability to feel or move from the lower chest down made it even harder.

It was good to go down to the physiotherapy department. There was a wide spectrum of patients, even though all were spinally-injured. People were from different backgrounds in terms of fitness, attitude to and stage of life, and wishes for the future. On top of this, there was an array of injuries. Admittedly, spinal cord injury defined the major long-term impairment. As well as coping with paralysis, there were complicating factors of spinal cord injury and the trauma process to contend with, such as weight loss, pressure sores, pain and muscle spasms. Spasms could be so bad in some patients that they would occasionally be chucked out of the wheelchair by them. Some patients had other injuries in addition to this. Not everyone there would be in-patients either. Some low-break patients might return to try walking with calipers. This is where calipers, equipment of straps and metal, are attached to the legs. The equipment holds the legs in a fixed position, without the need for leg muscle power to do so. These patients can mobilise short distances on their legs usually using crutches, after much training to perfect their balance and upper body strength. Hence the necessity of being a low-break patient to do this.

Rehabilitation for in-patients tends to be governed by the level of spinal cord injury. In general, there are certain expectations of what function you can achieve based on your level of injury. In general has to be a vague phrase, as people can do surprisingly better or worse than expected. A high tetraplegic person would not be expected to do a great deal of self-propulsion in a wheelchair and often be put in a chin-operated electrical wheelchair at an early stage. A low tetraplegic person should be able to self-propel in a manual chair and make some transfers, such as to bed or car, with help of others or equipment such as a sliding board. A paraplegic person, high or low, would be encouraged to do all transfers including to the floor, probably the hardest, and ideally without the need for help from others. Also, a paraplegic person would be expected to get up and down kerbs in their wheelchair, as pre-injury hand function remained and wheels could be controlled sufficiently to do wheelies with the front wheels off the ground. Then there are the incomplete breaks, both tetraplegic and paraplegic. They are a heterogeneous group, but a unifying feature is that the majority can walk in some fashion. As a result, the struggle to learn transfers and wheelchair skills is less needed….."lucky bastards," I say with joking jealousy. I think that calling them lucky must sound quite bizarre, as they are pretty damn unlucky to be in a Spinal Injuries Unit.

Doing wheelies sounds like good fun, but it's in fact pretty damned scary when you first have to control the wheelchair at its balance point on two back wheels. If ever tried, you might realise why I called the incomplete break patients "lucky bastards." And when you've experienced flying over backwards in the wheelchair after overdoing it to bang your head, it's even worse. "Lucky bastards" seems to ring even truer then when lamenting your situation. It's amazing, though, how time passes and you move on from what seems a terrible struggle at the time. As I am writing in the year 2000, I don't even think twice about wheeling off a kerb. It's no longer a trial and big deal; it's a part of life that doesn't worry me now. Because there has been such a transformation in how I live with wheelchair use in what almost seems like a blink of an eye to me on looking back, I wonder whether the same will happen in another eight years. I contemplate whether the major adaptation happens early and then it stays static, waiting for a decline as my body tires with my advancing years. It would only make sense for most improvement to occur early on. I hope it continues, though. I don't relish the decline, but who knows what I will want in another eight years?

Happiness is not all about physical ability, and sadness is not all about loss of ability. I should know that by now. Blimey, I've lost enough physical ability to realise that I still like life and have purpose despite my loss. I've still got those family members and friends close to me, and these relationships are at the crux of it. Some very good friends have come out of this experience to add to my life, too: people who I know make me laugh and smile, so much so that I often laugh when on my own and thinking back to past times behind. Some people must think that I'm psychiatric by the way that I behave sometimes. Better off a happy chappy than a Malcolm moody, though. Apologies to people called Malcolm. Just a figure of speech; no offence intended.

    I've digressed from the topic of my rehabilitation, although figuring out my attitude to life from then on was an important part of the adaptation process. As far as physical capability, though, I could initially only stick about an hour maximum in the gym. Slowly, time spent there increased. Officially, the sessions lasted two hours, both morning and afternoon. The first exercises to take part in were weight-training, balance, turning my body and touching my toes. A highlight of each session was the drinks' trolley coming around at half-time…no G and T, but still delicious and a major motivator to attend again when you're finding it tough. The taste buds have a good survival purpose in that case.

    Rehabilitation progressed. It was good to be interacting with people from my wheelchair height, rather than to be lying in bed focusing on the ceiling. As well as building up strength and learning necessary wheelchair skills, there were two standing frames in the physio department. These are contraptions, which paralysed people can lift themselves or be lifted into. A strap swung behind the bum area enables the person in it to stay standing and I must say that it was even better to stand than to sit. Full interaction was not possible, as I couldn't easily chat owing to my windpipe problem and tracheostomy, but nevertheless I valued standing and to be improving in a small way.

    It was very tiring to do the rehabilitation and also to see lots of visitors, but I needed both. Building my strength and learning new skills to enable independent functioning were undoubtedly essential, but family and friends were necessary tonic to kept spirits up. Some visitors were harder work than others, but I appreciated everyone's efforts and concern in visiting me.

    People in authority from medical school visited me at different stages from near the start. When I was at Frenchay Hospital and becoming very ill with my problematic breathing, visitors were limited. Some people were turned away to their dismay and ultimate concern about how ill I really was. If I was a visitor and not allowed to see someone in hospital because they were too ill, I would have thought that it was near the end. So I probably had been very close to dying when there. Fortunately, time had moved on from then. The bursar at medical school in London and his wife were a great support. Their visits were very uplifting for me, although the bursar's wife did try to convince me to take up the card game, bridge. I think that she knew that she was on a losing wicket there. I wasn't speaking at this stage, but my face didn't light up with interest. When she mentioned bridge, I would nod half-attentively and her husband would comment on how bridge was probably the last thing on my mind at that time. He was almost certainly right, although I appreciated that his wife was simply trying to get me interested again in something outside the hospital routine. This was very thoughtful of her and she didn't take offence when I showed no real interest. Kind and generous people indeed.

One of the consultant pathologists from my London medical school, St Bart's, also visited. He was extremely helpful and spoke of all the changes that they could do at Bart's to get me back, when the time was right. He was enthusiastic and dynamic. I hadn't really considered returning to medicine at this stage, as I was more preoccupied with coping with my current situation of simply surviving two hours in physiotherapy before being lifted on to the bed for an hour or so of rest before the afternoon session. It was nonetheless a boost to have this support. The optimism and unquestioning attitude towards my future capabilities by people at medical school made me never worry about obstacles to my return. Everyone was on my side. It would be more a question of whether I wanted to return to my studies, rather than whether people would let me do so. This pathology doctor also brought a crate of beer that was to be "hidden" deep in a locker near my bedside. It took a while before I wanted to indulge in alcohol again; wow, I must have really been sick! Before my beer buds recovered, visitors appreciated the opportunity for a tipple, when offered. That was if they were not driving, of course. I was more interested in a sugar rush and my relatives would frequently bring bags of sweets, so-called Pick 'n Mix, when they visited. I got a reputation for being the bloke with the good collection of sweets and this was another attraction, along with the booze, to bring people to my bedside.

When adept at wheelchair manoeuvring, people had to use shower chairs. These are self-propelled chairs with a hole in the centre of the seating area for the patient's bum, so that it can be used to go over toilets as well as into showers; in other words, the capability of doing bowels and washing in one chair. When I say adept at manoeuvring, in the case of the shower chair, it meant that you could balance sufficiently in the chair not to fall out. It's hardly as if you had to do stunts in it, such as wheelies up kerbs or even travel at great speeds. So balance didn't need to be brilliant to survive the shower chair experience. They were quite sturdy, not dangerously tippy and had little manoeuvrability. They served their basic purpose. I think that I would have needed to be on a psychiatric ward, if I decided to wheel anywhere other than near the toilet or shower area in a shower chair with towels draped over my naked form. It was quite a sight to behold, believe me.

Proper washes were made possible by the shower chair. I needed to be careful, though, because my tracheostomy tube caused me to choke when water went down it. Even so, it was so much better than having a flannel wash, despite the choking potential. Initially, I was supervised in the shower before being let loose on my own. In fact, I did once manage the amazing feat of falling out of a shower chair, while in a shower room on my own. Here's me, the bloke who was saying that they were sturdy non-tippy contraptions, impossible to fall out of. "Serves you right," I hear you say. Now I'll make the excuses. Essentially, one of the foot plates fell off the chair while I was in the shower and this led me to come forward out of the chair. Honest governor, that's how it really happened. Having fallen out, I had to lift myself along the floor to where there was an emergency call button, unlock the door and cover myself over having summoned help. Rather embarrassing to look up from the floor to the rescuers to explain the mess into which I had got myself. Very helpless and pathetic are the feelings that came to mind when this occurred. Still, it's not the worst thing that happened to me after all: just a small adventure along the way. Such is life in rehabilitation. My next time in a shower chair was somewhat more cautious than before, but you need to move on from these minor incidents. At least the nurses must find it funny telling each other about the latest exploits of certain patients.

Self-care was getting better. I was dressing myself, at last. This was initially not possible because my legs and hamstrings had become very tight after having been in bed for so long. This meant that I couldn't reach my toes with my hands, essential to put clothes on my lower body. After much leg stretching by my physio Kathy and basic activity on my part, I was finally able to bend fully at the waist and dress unaided. Use of the shower chair had enabled going over the toilet for doing one of life's essential functions. Us English always manage to get back to that subject. Even so, most people tend to be uncomfortable talking about that sort of thing. I don't think that I'm any different in getting embarrassed. Somehow, though, writing about it is easier than talking about it. I suppose that's because I don't have to look someone in the eye when writing. And what do we call it?.....toilet, loo, lavatory, karsy, WC......ablutions, business, toilet duty, number twos, defecation (very medical); the list gets worse, so I'll stop now. Whatever it's called, it is a tiresome ordeal for the spinally-injured person. The phrasing used does not alter the grave reality of what this function entails for someone spinally-injured. It does not change the intolerability of the hassle associated with it.

There are several reasons why going to the loo for many spinally-injured people is an annoyance. You usually need assistance in one form or another. Assistance can be in the form of suppositories, enemas or manual evacuation. I am a suppository and occasional manual evacuation man. What a chat up line: "Hey babe, I'm a suppository and occasional manual evacuation man. Fancy coming back to my place?" So bowels are a problem. Also, you can be over the toilet for ages. A mug of hot drink can help things along by a mechanism called the gastrocolic reflex but nonetheless the upshot of it is that you need to take plenty of good reading material with you. When first at the Spinal Injuries Unit, I, like most other new patients, couldn't use a shower chair. This meant that bowels were dealt with on the bed. Rolled onto one side, an inco pad would be placed under me to protect the bed and a nurse would deal with my bowels. It's quite degrading, but sadly it needed to be done. It's also not much fun for the nurses either. They must be quite relieved when a patient moves on to a shower chair, although as soon as someone progresses a new patient arrives. I take my hat off to the nurses. They have to do some unpleasant things and also be good at relating to patients at extremes of emotion. A fantastic group of people.

    I learned how to lift myself from my wheelchair to the bed without needing help, known as a bed transfer in Spinal Injuries Unit speak. This was thanks to dogged persistence on both my physiotherapist's and my own part. It would have been easy to get down in spirits with what an uphill struggle it was. The relationship that I had with Kathy, my physio, was invaluable. I would sometimes be jokingly stubborn about things that she would tell me to do. For example: "Tom, go on. Give it a try. Do this lift." "Says who?" I would retort. "Says me," Kathy would answer. "You and who's army?" Then I would try the lift, after an acknowledging look and smile. Anyone watching might have thought that it was unprofessional behaviour. It didn't, however, happen all the time and Kathy knew that I was keen to progress rather than mess around. Another game was to be the fastest to name the pop group, as the radio played in the physio department. Sad, I know, but needs must. Prefab Sprout used to be a regular guess of mine, usually wrong. I don't know why I guessed that group, but when it was them….did I laugh? Prefab Sprout was played, I think, just the once; not quite once in a blue moon, but nearly. I was only too aware not to make an embarrassing spectacle of either of us. We both were. Also, rehabilitation was the priority and we both knew that. Kathy was good at her job. She knew about rehabilitation and, probably more importantly, she helped me retain good humour when it would be easy to get low about life. The joking about was almost a necessary part of rehabilitation, a necessary release from the situation that I found myself in.

    It made a fantastic difference to my quality of life on the ward being able to do bed transfers. I can remember how tired I would get by lunchtime after the morning session in the physiotherapy department and before I could do bed transfers, I would yearn to get onto my bed. It was like torture to see all those who could do it, as they rested and regained their strength at half-time of the day's activities. It felt like a big imposition on the nurses to ask them to give me a hand every lunchtime. Also, a rule on lifting patients came into effect while I was at Odstock. The rule was that if nurses were to lift patients above a certain weight, it was at their own risk. The result of this was that if I wanted to get on my bed, the nurses either risked injuring their backs or they used a hoist machine to minimise this risk. A hoist was a very time-consuming clumsy device, so I would rarely ask to be moved to my bed at lunchtime. Instead I would lean over the edge of my bed from my wheelchair as a compromise, while envying those who had the joy of being able to get on their beds on their own and fully stretch out their backs. So when I joined those who could lie on the bed at midday, it was a joy. It took ages to regain my stamina to any sustainable level and you need rest, as well as exercise and nutrition, to get it back. I had lost almost five stones in weight in the month immediately after the accident. It would take at least two years after the accident before I felt that I was approaching a good level of fitness. Weeks to lose it, years to recover it.

Chapter 10

When did I realise that I had been badly and permanently injured?

There was never a time when I suddenly thought that I would never walk again, that I would never have the same freedom with my bladder and bowels previously taken for granted. It was more of a gradual realisation. It was a very confusing process in the early stages after the accident. This was probably contributed by head injury, low oxygen blood levels as a result of my windpipe narrowing, being in the foreign surroundings of a hospital, and drugs with sedatory and hallucinogenic side effects. And I'm not talking about recreational use, officer! There might also have been an element of denial on my part. It was as if I had woken from a dream, not a good one I stress, to find myself in this situation. It almost had to be a dream because the terrible situation in which I found myself seemed so unreal. To add to this illusion of it all being a dream was the fact that I couldn't initially remember that I had had an accident. There was a slow recollection of events over a long period of time. It took a few months for me to start to remember the events that happened on that fateful skiing holiday. The façade of everything being imagined slowly dwindled as the details of what had happened came back to me.

    It was almost fascinating how memories of what had happened came back gradually. I would remember things in bits. First, I could remember getting to the ski-resort by coach, our apartment and collecting the ski equipment in Val d'Isere town on the first day. Next I could remember the first morning's skiing on the nursery slopes, then the funicular to get to the top of the mountain and the afternoon's skiing on the harder slopes. After this, there was an evening meal spent with a group of us, then the hotel, then walking home with my three friends. We were sliding along the road in skid manoeuvres using our feet on the ice. Rather ironically, I can remember myself hanging back a little and doing less impetuous slides. Then we reached near the apartment block. I can remember messing about in a stream, splashing water. We were excited to be on holiday with a childlike enthusiasm. Then the use of mats for tobogganing down the slope was suggested. Ellie said that she had had enough. Then the remaining trio, Andrew, Ian and me, went up the slope with a mat. Just a little way up the slope was all that was done. "How can such a small distance up a slope cause so much destruction?" I would wonder to myself, almost incredulously, in trying to come to terms with how my body had been wrecked. "How could I be in this situation, if I only went a short distance up a ski-slope with a toboggan mat? It seemed such an innocent thing to do." I can remember getting on the left front, with Andrew on the right front and Ian on the back. I can remember the mat sliding quickly down the slope and voices shortly before impact. Fortunately, I haven't remembered the impact yet. Let's hope that I never do. All these memories came back to me over years. I have often wondered why it took so long. I'm sure that it is partially protective. I would have probably been overwhelmed to have remembered these details at a very early stage. My energies so soon after injury were obviously channeled into other tasks necessary for survival.

    During the first few months at Odstock Hospital, I would see some patients begin walking after their time of bed-rest. For some reason, I was expecting to be doing that in a few months time. It was strange to be thinking that, while at the same time being aware of no feeling or movement below my lower chest level. This awareness was somehow blunted, though. I wasn't sure whether something magical happened when you were recovered enough to make the transition from being in bed to being put in a wheelchair. Admittedly, there is a thing called spinal shock, where function might improve significantly when this type of shock resolves. But spinal shock usually only lasts a few weeks, such that if you have no improvement after that time a dramatic improvement is highly unlikely. I had not seen my scans, but apparently they were convincing evidence there that my impairment would probably not resolve spontaneously. When you are confused, in an unfamiliar situation in hospital and seeing so many different and unusual things, you cling to hope. No one ever actually uninvitedly said that I would not walk again. I think that this was helpful. I was able to work out my predicament in my own way and time and after a certain amount of rehabilitation. There was definitely denial on my part and I am sure that it had its purpose.

     My adaptation was such a gradual thing. It takes years, rather than weeks and months, to get your head around your situation properly. Years on, as I reflect on my experiences, I am still learning to live with my condition and work out where my life is going. I suppose that everyone has to do that, whether physically impaired or not. How can I communicate it best? I will never get over what has happened to me. Whatever my background is, the physical insults will never go away. I have had to learn to live a new life. The fact that I was a student doctor when the accident happened made no real difference to my recovery. This was especially so in the early stages. I was initially very confused and there might have been things like denial clouding the picture for me further. Practical aspects of wheelchair use and gaining physical capabilities, rather than understanding what was wrong with me, was the priority then. My medical knowledge wouldn't have changed things, and most of the patients seemed to have as good an understanding of what was wrong as was necessary in any case. The challenge ahead was not obviously, if at all, different to any other patient in the Spinal Injuries Unit. It was about finding out where my life was heading with this newly acquired difficulty, discovering my strengths and deciding what I wanted to do.

Chapter 11

Raising money: a past challenge of mine achieved by others; generosity abounds

Andrew and other medical school friends organised a fundraising event at my London Medical School, while I continued to undergo my hospital rehabilitation. It was to get money for myself and a local spinal charity based at Odstock Hospital called INSPIRE. INSPIRE stands for Integrated Spinal Rehabilitation and produces technologies to improve the lives of people with spinal cord injury. Thirty people agreed to take part in the sponsored event, the Fourteen Peaks Challenge. Completing the Fourteen Peaks, a feat that I had achieved a year previously, is dreadfully difficult and doing so is very reliant on the weather. There were several obstacles to success: the willingness of people to sponsor, the weather, and the people taking part being able to complete it even if the weather was good.

The generosity of people to sponsor the event was amazing. People who didn't even know me would give sponsorship, sometimes large. However, it was not so much the amount raised that struck me, although that was strikingly impressive with thousands of pounds being raised. It was more that there were so many people behind my recovery and giving me every chance to make a success of my new life. Fortunately, the weather was on good behaviour and the majority of participants finished the challenge. When I remember how difficult the Fourteen Peaks is to complete, I was astounded that so many did so. I would not scorn anyone in any way, if they didn't do it. There were no failures in my eyes. Everyone had given it a go and they all had been an inspiration to me by doing so. And it wasn't just those that attempted the challenge that were involved. There were also the organisers, minibus drivers, helpers at the different checkpoints, sponsors, the chairman of the charity INSPIRE and many more that made it all possible. The supportive spirit of having so many involved in the event was truly astonishing, truly strengthening for me. I was now able to afford a lightweight wheelchair from the proceeds of this event and this was so much easier to use than a heavy NHS one.

Equipment does indeed make a difference because you can't achieve things with just motivation. You need support in many ways to supplement it.

It was also fantastic that a charity based at the Spinal Injuries Unit had some useful funds coming its way. My accident had been a significant event and significant efforts were being made to conquer its consequences. What a brilliant fundraising effort it had been. My heartfelt thanks went out to everyone.

Chapter 12

A trip to Salisbury in the Spinal Injuries Unit minibus

Progress at the Spinal Injuries Unit is a funny old process. Even the tiniest change can be considered by the individual patient to be major progress. Simple things like staying out of bed in your wheelchair for an hour more than usual, doing a pressure-lift on your wheelchair wheels for thirty seconds instead of twenty or, to be crude as I feel the need sometimes, managing to have your bowels open after only half an hour. Wow! I've knocked twenty minutes of my record and with the use of only two suppositories. Suppositories are drugs allowed in my paraplegic bum Olympics. It is such a hassle. It consumes so much time. Long-term, it's probably one of the worst aspects of my injury. It's a life sentence to prolonged toilet visits. Bowels are only worse than bladder, though, if you don't wet yourself too often in public. Fortunately I don't, fingers and legs crossed. But it's still a worry that hasn't gone away with time, since being sentenced to a chair. It sounds a harsh sentence, but it's certainly not the electric chair of death penalty notoriety and life does indeed go on. These stresses are mentally wearing, though, and they add up to make life as a spinally-injured person in a wheelchair that much harder than someone from the outside might imagine. Life is, nevertheless, still fulfilling, despite these added burdens and I find myself appreciating what I have got some much more than I did before. Ambivalence seems to abound.

   Here I'm back to talking about toilets but the reality is that toilets have a bigger role in my life if I add up the time devoted to them now. Into the bargain I need a bigger roll…toilet roll, that is! I might make cras and sometimes feeble jokes about the difficulty of going to the toilet, but this is only to try to lighten up my situation and the knowledge that doing it at a near-normal pace again would be heaven. It might even been as big a deal as walking. You will almost certainly not think of paraplegia in this light, unless you have had close contact with the experience of it or have endured it. Most uninitiated people see the wheelchair, but very few see the bladder and the bowels. I hear you, reader, asking why I'm rambling on about toilet visits, when this chapter is about Salisbury, more famous for a cathedral with a tall spire and a market square rather than for public conveniences. The struggle for progress was my point. I had reached the stage where I could go to Salisbury for an afternoon. An afternoon of non-hospital life was really appealing. The feelings that I had were a bit like those that I remember having before going on a school field trip when a youngster. The excitement and my innocence of the outside world were almost childlike in nature. I would be lying if I said that there was no apprehension. Necessarily, it was a trip done with lots of therapists, physio- and occupational- rather than psycho-therapists, to help us nervous patients cope with the outing.

The minibus had a chair-lift at its backdoor and the chairs were ushered in one by one. It wasn't quite Noah's Arc escaping the hospital and the weather was fine, too, so no floods lay in our way. Once in the minibus, the chairs were secured to the floor with straps to limit sliding and casualties of unexpected falls. The journey was a little bumpy, but I held on in a white-knuckle fashion. It was great to arrive in Salisbury city centre and that wasn't because my hands were tired from holding on. It was simply the taste of freedom that refreshed me. When out of the minibus, I savoured the fresh air that wasn't tarnished by the sight and smells of hospital. I was back in the real world again. When my physio Kathy and a friend of mine went to a tea house, it was fantastic. I had a hot chocolate and cake and at long last I was experiencing some of the delights of being out of hospital again. I had not experienced the real world like this for quite a few months, although it seemed even longer than that to me. I could even throw in the cliché that it seemed like a lifetime ago. There, I've done it.

It's difficult to communicate how good it felt. I could spell how as hoooooow to emphasise it, but that misses the point. It's probably a similar feeling to coming out of prison after a long sentence; not that I've ever been in prison to compare! No thank you. One lengthy hospital term, however good the staff, is enough. This momentary taste of freedom from the hospital institution did me a lot of good because it was great to be in a real life situation where the wheelchair rehabilitation was not the main concentration. We went into Sainsburys, a real supermarket, to buy some crisps and sweets, and then into real shops to look for other things to buy. You truly regress to a dependent person, when you're in hospital for a long time. It was almost unbelievable to be out of the hospital. It was like being a kiddie, when you're finding it so amazing to be experiencing new things that you have to call them real to reaffirm them as believable. I was back in the land of the "normal", but I had much to relearn. It felt good, though, and gave me the appetite for more.

Chapter 13

Further trips outside

My next adventure was a night out with my physio and occupational therapist, Kathy and Lisa. We were off to a nearby pub for an evening meal. We went by a wheelchair taxi, as I couldn't transfer myself from a wheelchair to the car seat yet. We set off having to take with us my portable suction machine, a lifeline to the outside with it being a mechanical suction device that I used to remove secretions from my tracheostomy tube if I became "bubbly." Hardly romantic but the suction device was a necessity. Suctioning was to be avoided if at all possible and, if needed, to be done preferably out of sight. The challenge was not to put fellow diners at the pub off their food.

Our destination was the Victoria and Albert pub in a village near Salisbury. I got on really well with both my therapists. I could even dare call them friends at this stage, but we needed to maintain some degree of professionalism. It was a great joy to be going out for the night and, when the three of us were together, all pretence was abandoned. The drive was as uneventful as can be: no cracked heads at least, despite a cramped taxi. The next challenge was to get into the pub. It sounds easy, especially when not drunk, but the entrance was through a couple of doors at a sharp angle to each other. It took lots of pushing and shoving, laughter and several attempts at different angles of attack to get in. We did it, though; and, my goodness, it was worth it. A pleasant country pub with fantastic food, beer and real log fire was the prize.

I perused the menu with glee at my further found freedom. It was not a reflection on the hospital being particularly bad. The hospital was as good as it could reasonably be. Even so, when I touched the outside world again, it reminded me of the liberties which I had lost for a substantial time and which I still hadn't fully regained. This night was an exception to my prevailing routine. I treasured it. I hope that I never forget how lucky I am, when enjoying an evening out with friends. "You never appreciate something until it's gone" is an old saying that certainly rings true. I was tasting not just great food that evening. I was also tasting good company in relaxed surroundings, the warmth of a cosy pub, and the freedom to choose what I wanted to eat and drink. I was an inmate released on good behaviour. What a feeling. Perhaps a second saying should be "remember to appreciate something now that it's back." Call me an old wife with stupid tales, if you like. As I write this book, I have slipped into a routine in which life is very busy with little time for relaxation and active reflection. It's so easy to get wrapped up in my troubles and challenges ahead, and forget about where I've come from along my road of recovery. At least now it's written, I can remind myself by simply reading about it if need be.

The evening was a great success. Fortunately for Kathy and Lisa, my muteness prevented them from having to listen to my far from brilliant collection of jokes. Indeed, sometimes silence can be golden. I returned to hospital safely under the escort of my two capable guardians. They didn't put their backs out or have any other injury relevant to a Spinal Injuries Unit in the process, so everyone was happy. I got back to my bed-space having completed another mission. I was beginning to learn that there would be many "mission difficults" along the way. There would rarely be "mission impossibles," though, unless I wanted something daftly impratical like, for example, wanting to be a paratrooper, not that I wanted that in any case. The closest that I'd get to being a para is being a paraplegic. I think that what I've learned is that while you can surprise yourself by what you achieve and so shouldn't set rigid limitations, at the same time you should be realistic about what you might be able to achieve.

Now that this evening had gone well, I could go out to pubs at weekends with my family. There are lots of great pubs in the countryside near the hospital. Over a period of a few weeks, a comprehensive knowledge of the local pubs was gained. It was always a pleasure to go out for lunch. The toilet accessibility was usually far from satisfactory. On most occasions, I would have to wee into a urine bag strapped to my leg and empty it into a urine jug under the table. Usually, my mum, bless her, would smuggle the jug under her raincoat to the pub toilet. We would joke about her being tackled by the owner for looking suspicious, causing an awful mess. She's a generous good-humoured woman, if ever she needs telling.

Another night out was spent at a social club on the outskirts of Salisbury. About ten of us patients went with a few nurses from the ward. It was great to get out of the hospital in a big group setting, something that I hadn't really done since my accident. The jukebox played songs of our choice. I was still lacking in voice as a result of my throat problem, but this didn't stop me enjoying the outing. There was less pressure on me making a major contribution to the evening's jollity. The sounds of the song "Everybody hurts" by REM filtered through the background noise of conversation. I sat there and contemplated for the duration of the song what I and the other fellow patients had been through so far and were still going through. The song somehow gave me permission to feel sad, not that I needed much of an excuse in any case. Sometimes, though, you actually need to be told that you should hurt, and that it's normal, and that other people feel hurt, too. The song and situation conveyed this well. The moment had been seized. There was certainly much evidence of lives interrupted and misery inflicted. I was not alone. Most of us there had struggled to wonder what was going to go right when everything in life had seemed so wrong, and almost unfair.

I had tears in my head. I still couldn't believe what had happened to me, expecting someone to tell me that my body would be alright again. There were so many others in a similar situation. Surely not everyone would be alright. My denial was not diminishing easily. Hope, however irrational, needed to remain. My hidden melancholy and wish to beat the pain of tragedy was all too apparent to me. This sadness truly had a healing purpose for me. Seeing the suffering of others, indeed a collective of badly wounded individuals, prevented me from being alone. However damaged we were, the group was still out to have fun. Life was not going to defeat us yet. I had to move on with my life, rather than just reflect on what had happened. I needed to hang on to my love for fun and living. However my body was, I could still have this. My contribution to the evening was selecting the lively sound of the song "Let's talk about sex, baby" by Salt n' Pepa to the groans of "Who put this on?", as I sheepishly laughed.

I felt safe with people that I knew well. A fact was pervasively apparent. At this stage, I needed to be with others to survive the non-hospital environment. The world outside seemed an exciting, yet inaccessible and almost intangible, place to discover. There was a fear to be without an able-bodied person outside the hospital. This made me realise that I was truly institutionalised, dependent on the solace and security of the hospital. When you are at that stage, it's difficult to imagine making the transition from hospital to home. It's all very well going to a pub a couple of miles from and so within easy reach of the hospital, one of the restrictions on distance being anxiety about the tracheostomy tube. It was the thought of being back home, which was about sixty miles from the hospital, that was truly terrifying. It is the people with you that bring you through. They didn't show that they were terrified, thankfully. Nor did I, if I'm honest. Just as well one doesn't share all the worries. There's a lot to be said for blissful ignorance sometimes.

Chapter 14

A night in the adapted self-contained flat of the Spinal Injuries Unit

There was a general rule in the Spinal Injuries Unit that each patient had to spend a night in the hospital's specially adapted apartment before being allowed home. There were two bedrooms, a kitchen and a living room area within the flat. The object of this ordeal was to make sure that the patient could survive off the ward, having to cook, make the bed and do his or her self-care. It was a good way of determining whether the patient needed further rehabilitation, certain adaptations done to their home that were not already apparent or even if support from a carer was necessary.

My mum and dad came down to do this exercise with me. This wasn't against the rules, since they would be at home when I would go there for the first time. My mum is very maternal and it is difficult to stop her doing things. As I was supposed to attempt to undertake some activities as part of this exercise, my mum needed a certain degree of self-control to stop herself doing things for me. Even so, I didn't insist on doing everything. We had a tasty evening meal, watched a bit of television and finally retired to our respective bedrooms. The flat was not ideal, but this was probably because it was unfamiliar. I had got so used to the ward layout that any change was testing. Hence the reason people have to have a night here before returning home.

We managed to get through the night without trouble and in the morning I cooked bacon, eggs, tomatoes and toast. I didn't drop sizzling saucepans on my lap and the breakfast was delicious, even if I say so myself. The flat is next to the physio and occupational therapy departments and there were lots of therapists about that morning. They all commented on the wonderful smell of breakfast and it was indeed fantastic. This hoop through which I had jumped gave me a passport to go home for the weekend. Rehabilitation and general recovery had been extremely stressful so far, but major progress could now be actively seen. Home was on the horizon, even if only for a weekend.

Chapter 15

A trip back home

I had learned how to get in and out of cars, and this meant that a trip home was on the cards. A home visit had been made already by Kathy and Lisa to check out my parent's house for suitability to accommodate my wheelchair. The plan was for me to go home on a Saturday morning and return on Sunday afternoon. It must have been September 1992 when I was first allowed home. It was about six months after the accident itself. What a feeling to be returning for the first time to a place with memories of before my accident. I had mixed feelings, which ranged from excitement to trepidation, and almost terror. I didn't know what to expect my reaction to be. Since being in hospital, I had not seen many people from my parents' village. It was going to be strange to see these faces, especially now that I felt dramatically altered and much more vulnerable both physically and emotionally. I wasn't sure whether there would be gaggles of village folk through whom I would have to be escorted to the house like some famous person. Like it or not, I was infamous to many people now. I joked on the journey in the car about this imagined struggle like a celebrity through crowds to the house front door. This helped ease the tensions a little.

The journey home took a couple of hours. My dad was the chauffeur, with my brother Ali in attendance on the back seat. I sat in the front passenger seat. It was a big adventure for me and my family. The trips back and forth from Bristol to Salisbury, which my family had already made, must have been very wearing for them. They must have done the journey more than a hundred times already. But this time it was different. I was in the car. This journey, probably inconsequential for most, was a major step for me. I would be about two hours away from the safe haven of the Spinal Injuries Unit. When you've been used to a place for a long time, it's scary to have a break from that routine. I must say that I did feel extremely dependent. I relied on my family to get me through this period at home, despite the fact that I had already done a lot of rehabilitation. It would take a long time before I could be confident about looking after myself properly.

Just getting through a day was a struggle at this time. I would still get tired if in the wheelchair for prolonged periods. My transfers from the wheelchair to bed, car and armchair required a lot of effort, and I didn't have it in me to do things such as cooking and other tasks on a regular basis. I could do basic things like washing and dressing myself, but most other things were beyond me at this stage. It may sound a bit pathetic and lazy, but I had very little stamina. I also wasn't particularly practised at coordinating myself when cooking and so risking me getting burned, scalded or even electrocuted. "What a liability!," I hear people say. I do not disagree. I was certainly a hazard and probably not only to myself. If I was doing the cooking, my family had better check that fire damage was on their house insurance policy. It would take me a long time to develop proper fitness and coordination; and I mean months going on years.

Thank goodness to have such a supportive family set-up, which enabled me to progress gradually. It would have been very difficult to fend for myself. There was a need to have people doing things for me while my capabilities were restricted until I became fitter. By having a family that could do a certain amount of things for me, I could channel my energies to coping with the new challenge of trips home without exhaustion. It meant that I could enjoy the trip, rather than feeling that it was an unachievable hurdle. A secret to my recovery was to take on one goal at a time, instead of trying to conquer the world in one go. Gradual small steps make a large one in the end, with less chance of injury or major disappointment when things don't go right.

It was a really pleasant time away from hospital. The trip by car was along roads over the Mendip Hills and there were beautiful views to be seen on a clear day. On this particular journey, Glastonbury Tor could even be seen in the distance to the West, and lush green fields and hills were in most directions. Dad had kindly made a foam cushion to fit the front car seat, as his car had very hard bucket seats. Every so often I would do a lift with my hands on the sides of the car seat to relieve pressure on my bum area and prevent skin marking because of my lack of sensation there. The portable suctioning machine was in the boot of the car, in case my tracheostomy tube became frothy with secretions. If this happened, a suitable parking spot would be found, so that I could shove a suction catheter down the tube to clear it of secretions. There was no rushed panic if this needed to be done because it was routine for me, but it could appear quite gruesome to an outsider not used to it. The journey seemed to go swimmingly, despite the very occasional pressure lift or need to suction as interruptions.

    At home was a steep drive to negotiate. The rest of my close family came out to greet me on our arrival. To my relief, there was no fan club of villagers. My dad had made a wooden ramp to help get over the step at the front door and we managed to get in without incident. Once in the house, there was the kitchen, dining room, downstairs toilet and sitting room. All rooms were accessible, except for the downstairs toilet. The sitting room had been made into two rooms by having curtains in the centre to divide the room in two. It was now part sitting room, part my makeshift bedroom for the time-being. At one end of the room was a sofa, chairs and, of course, the ever-necessary television. At the other end was a bed, which had been moved downstairs. On the window-sill behind the bed, there were separate photos of my siblings and me graduating, mine when I collected my BSc degree in 1991. There was also a family photo of me, my mum, sister and brothers. The curtains and wooden rail in the centre of room, put in place by my dad, ensured my privacy. It felt quite symbolic that behind the curtains lay both my past and present life. Behind these curtains, I was to start my life away from hospital, my new life of worldly wheelchair use.

Chapter 16

What did the first weekend home entail?

The inaccessibility of the downstairs toilet meant that my bedroom area in the sitting room also had to be my bathroom. All this mentioning of different rooms makes it awfully confusing, especially when there are three rooms in one. Did all this bode well for a successful trip home? My makeshift bedroom, also being a bathroom, would be possible with improvisation. Washes were with a bowl and flannel. Bladder care was a combination of urosheaths draining into urine leg-bags, and occasional use of an intermittent catheter to empty my bladder fully. Bowels involved glycerine suppositories and inco pads on the bed, due to no commode being available. Now I expect that the importance of the curtains for my privacy is even more apparent to the reader. Bowel management was quite an indignity. Everyone should really be given the dignity of adequate and non-degrading toilet facilities. The lack of them for the time-being was a small price that I was willing to pay in order to get home. I greatly valued escaping the hospital at weekends and sometimes the best has to be made of a situation.

  My mum is an excellent cook, so the food at home was a treat. You see, there are some big benefits to being the sickly one. I saw my old cat, a long-haired senile black and white creature called Oliver, who was twelve years old when I first came home. He's a strange moggy and it was good to see that certain things hadn't changed as he gave his customary meow. He's deaf, and so the meow is rather out of tune. And when I say that he's senile, I'm not joking. It's sadly true. He sees another cat out of the window and jumps off the windowsill to go outside. Halfway to the cat flap, he forgets what he's doing and has to turn to come back to the windowsill. He's now almost twenty and his dementia has been progressive. He is so stupid. He can't even use a cat flap now, even if someone opens it for him. That's far too much said about Oliver. It was just good to have reinforced the memories, which I had had of home while in hospital, by experiencing them at first-hand. It could easily have been to the contrary and had been quite traumatic to be reminded of what life was like before the accident. But, fortunately, that wasn't the case.

It was great to be at home with my close family, who had visited me in hospital so very often. We now had our own privacy. We were almost living our chosen way of life again. This was in contrast to the feeling, which I had had in hospital, that I was not really living my life. It wasn't as bad as it could have been in hospital because I was able to see people who I cared about and vice versa quite frequently. The staff were also vital to my sanity by being exceptional people in general. But there was an inescapable truth that I was trying to get to a level of function in hospital, such that I could be let out to attempt to live my new life outside. The hospital existence was where one struggled to gain some sort of health. The aim was to escape as soon as practically possible, but I didn't want to rush it and leave too soon. It would be essential to have the basic tools for general living, as well as for wheelchair independence, before departure. Even so, no matter how much preparation is made, the proper rehabilitation only starts when you leave the hospital.

The first step had been made towards this. I had survived about thirty hours away from the Spinal Injuries Unit. Was I becoming a person of the community again? Maybe I was, but a blatantly obvious fact was that I was always going to be very different. My almost celebrity status at my London medical school with all the fundraising and exceptional concern and support had been evidence of this. I hadn't taken it all in, though. However, within all this was almost an obligation to my close friends and family to be a good man. I wanted to be as good a man as I could possibly be. I did not just feel obliged. I actually really wanted to make something special out of my life. I very much wanted to give something back. I was in a unique position of being able to be in a respected position in society as a doctor, yet also to appear vulnerable and to have scars of how unfair life can be. You could almost call these scars my medals, and I wanted to get to the point where I could wear them with pride rather than consider them in a negative fashion. I had a lot to be thankful for. My brain was fully functioning despite having had a significant head injury. Also, if I could regain my speech, as well as there being much less frustration for me, I would have even more potential to get on with what I thought I was good at, especially now. This was to communicate with people about life, not only as a doctor to patient but also simply as a person who has endured dreadful things.

    I had experienced enough difficult times to be able to empathise with most other people. A keen listening ear, non-judgemental attitude and open-mind are the necessary ingredients. Experience of having to adapt to my situation and having people visit me at extremes of emotion had given me some wisdom. It taught me what was important and also not to take someone simply on their external appearance. Everyone has hidden aspects and usually something special about them and something to offer. Much lies behind the curtains of someone's physical shell and the only way to find out is by the person letting you in, sometimes with you needing to ask the right questions. Never assume, simply ask. As a result of my accident, I was indeed learning a lot more than just about how to live with spinal cord injury. My attitudes, as well as my physical capabilities, were being shaped.

Chapter 17

Where was I going to live when I left hospital?

When considering where to live, I had to think whether I could cope on my own. I also needed to consider who I would like to have near me. At this stage, I didn't envisage me coping without any difficulty and in all honesty I thought that I would always have reliance on people for help. An initial suggestion of modifications to my parents' house and a stair-lift installation was finally thought to be far less than ideal. Realistically I didn't think that there would be anything ideal, but there had to be something better. There was, in fact, a derelict cottage next door to my parents' house, which belonged to the County Council. My parents had suggested that they might be able to enquire about buying it. It seemed like a good idea and possibly the best solution. I would be independent and have privacy, while at the same time having people on hand for support if needed. My parents would also be more comfortable with this situation, rather than having me miles away. I thought that it was a good idea and my parents were very happy to look into it further.

Having approached the Council about the cottage, it was agreed that my parents should be able to buy it, although it still had to go through all the appropriate channels first. These things usually take a few months, but it was attempted to speed them up when my situation of being in hospital waiting for a home was made apparent. Even so, it did take months rather than weeks to be sorted out properly. At least, when my parents had acquired the cottage, we could focus on trying to get the cottage equipped for my needs. As mentioned, the cottage was derelict which meant that it required a bit more than a stair-lift and a couple of ramps to be fitted. The whole cottage needed to be gutted and even a new roof erected. Essentially, there was a shell of a cottage, in which there had to be everything I needed to live independently.

This was going to be some job to do. How would we go about it, now that my parents had bought the cottage? In came my oldest brother Andrew who is an architect and he had kindly offered to draw up plans for the building work. He, my dad and I sat down to discuss what was needed in the house. He then went away and devised a layout. There were two floors to the cottage and within it there should be ideally a sitting room, kitchen, study area, bedroom and bathroom. The final drawings had an open plan downstairs, consisting of study, sitting room and kitchen. At the back, facing eastwards, a conservatory was proposed. Upstairs was the bedroom and an en-suite bathroom, with a wheel-in shower and a bath. There was also a spiral staircase for the walkers to get upstairs. We were very limited by space available and a spiral staircase took up the least room. There was going to be a wheelchair lift for me at the side of the main room. This would be manually operated by me and counterweighted to allow ease of operation. Sliding doors, instead of standard push-pull ones, were an essential space saving method in the plans. The general idea was to have a functional cottage, which would be easy for me to use but at the same time have it aesthetically pleasing. This is obviously easier to achieve when you have a shell of a house in which to have a design of your own making from scratch, rather than to make bodge-job changes to a house designed primarily for non-wheelchair users.

Perhaps, when talking about the house design, I should call the sitting room the living room. After all every room is the sitting room for me because I sit in every room. Oh, who cares? If I'm not careful, I could confuse myself with trying to be too factually correct. I agree with the importance of correct wording because it can reflect and affect attitudes. You can, however, overdo it sometimes, especially when it has no bearing on things. It's rather a poor attempt at humour in any case. Let's call it a sitting room. You fret too much about what to say, until someone often rightly says, "Get a life!"

Each time my brother Andrew came up with a new plan, we moved around it with a cut-out scale version of my wheelchair. This would tell us whether there were any disasters in the plan, such as not being able to get through the front door or turn into the lift, before the plan was finalised and building had begun. The building work would be starting in early 1993 and the completion date was May 1993. I still had much to do in hospital: complete the necessary rehabilitation, tackle the speech and tracheostomy tube problem, which probably entailed major throat surgery, and decide on what to do with my life.

    Getting back to college hadn't even really entered my mind yet. Even if I decided to go to college, did I want to return to my medical studies? Which medical school? was another question. London wasn't ideal, despite having fantastic support of friends and key staff from medical school up the Smoke. London is bad enough to survive in, even when not in a wheelchair. It was going to be a struggle wherever I went, so I needed to make it as easy as possible for myself. Besides location, I didn't know if I would be able to manage this medical school lark. I didn't even know whether I would be self-sufficient on leaving hospital. I would need a lot of help on initial hospital discharge. There were many uncertainties. All I could concentrate on now was daily living in hospital and waiting on what happened to my throat. Much depended on the outcome of this. I felt that life was far too complicated at the time, as well as my mind being still unsure about the whole reason behind my life. Until my voice returned, I couldn't properly think about my future and my work. I needed to do lots of contemplation about both life and my role in it. I had plenty of time ahead in hospital in which to do this. Even so, the prospect of a comfortable accessible home was something to help ease the strain.

Chapter 18

Unplanned neck operation: the tracheal scar tissue lives

Some tracheostomy tubes consist of two tubes, an inner and outer tube. The inner slides snugly inside the outer one and is locked in place by twisting it at its end once it is fully advanced. I preferred these types of tubes because the inner tube could be removed and cleaned thoroughly clear of gunky mucus without needing to remove the outer tube from its position in the neck. If a tube is fenestrated, there is a window in the arch of both inner and outer tubes. A greater proportion of air can bypass the tube to resonate the vocal cords if a fenestrated tube is used. The fenestration makes it both easier to speak and to breathe conventionally. Speech occurs only on the presumption that the windpipe is not blocked above the tube. I had a fenestrated two-piece tracheostomy tube. Sadly, my windpipe blockage meant that I couldn't take full advantage of the fenestration for voice production or conventional breathing.

Things had nonetheless been going swimmingly, as far as tube maintenance had been concerned. Despite deliberately trying not to think this and tempt fate further for my nuisance of a neck, a little problem cropped up. I couldn't remove the inner tube from the main outer bit one morning. I tried quite hard and eventually summoned help from one of the nurses. The nurse couldn't figure out what was going on and when the ward doctor was unable to cure the problem, he decided to ask the ear, nose and throat specialist to come. Also, probably the ward doctor didn't want to get too involved with the patient infamous for neck complications. Better to get some expert help.

I had already been assessed by a consultant throat surgeon from London and by one from Salisbury. The consultant in Salisbury had therefore met me before, when he was asked to take a look at my misbehaving tube. He arrived with a friendly greeting smile. I returned the smile with an additional raising of the eyebrows. He had another member of his team, his registrar, with him. Having inspected and twiddled the tube, he agreed with our conclusions that the inner tube wasn't shifting. More important was to find out why this was so. Each attempt to move the inner tube resulted in a pain, mainly referred to my upper jaw and ear area on both sides, which restricted further movement. Out came the flexible laryngoscope. This is a very thin floppy telescope, which is used to look in areas inaccessible to the unaided eye. He advanced it down my tracheostomy tube, as he peered through the viewfinder. He had the answer. The scar tissue, which had obstructed my airway above the tracheostomy tube, was the culprit. It was now growing through the window in the tracheostomy tube from above. Hence this scar tissue was preventing the inner tube from being pulled out. The surgeon explained the situation. A general anaesthetic was needed to change the tube, since, despite all efforts, it couldn't be taken out without severe pain. Undisturbed by this, I agreed placidly. In any case, there was no disagreement to have. It had to be done and the surgeon would rather have avoided an operation if at all possible. I hadn't eaten or drunk anything for a while, so off we went to the operating theatre.

The room where the intravenous line is inserted and anaesthetic given was upon me. As I lay flat on the trolley, I gazed up at the clock on the wall. The anaesthetic was injected into my bloodstream and I felt a warm feeling, as my head went muzzy and the clock numbers blurred. It was a really pleasant feeling, like a feeling of embarking on a very satisfying sleep. The next memory is of waking up in the recovery room. It's a strange experience when you feel yourself become progressively more conscious in quite quick steps. It's the most rapid experience of a transition to a sober state that one will ever feel. I had had my general anaesthetic buzz….not that I was an addict, a general anaesthetic junky, although this might be questioned at the end of the year after many operations with there being another unplanned operation or two. Such is the unpredictability of human recovery.

Once not talking gobbledygook, the journey to the ward was thought safe…not that I needed to ask for directions or anything like that. The upshot of the morning's events was that a new tube was in place now and the unplanned trip to theatre meant that physiotherapy was not on the agenda for the rest of the day, as I needed to recover from the general anaesthetic. This patient goes to extraordinary lengths to avoid physiotherapy. Boy, he must be suffering badly down there in the physiotherapy gym! At least, I could jokingly wind up Kathy, my physiotherapist, that her fitness regime had driven me to these extremes.

Chapter 19

Legal challenges

My father had contacted various solicitors to discuss my case. As it turned out, our case would need to be funded out of our own pockets because we were not allowed legal aid for help with solicitor payments. This was because the case had to be conducted abroad. We did get a free first hour consultation, though! Should I be thankful for very small mercies? I probably should be, in order to prevent extreme cynicism on my part.

  The relevant information had been passed on to a firm of solicitors, which my dad had selected as suitable. Now that I had been going home for weekends, my dad arranged an appointment for us to meet two lawyers from the chosen firm. The purpose of the meeting was to discuss how best to move on with the case. My dad drove me to the very plush offices in Bristol and, after a short wait, we were ushered into a room with the two solicitors.

  It must have been in about October 1992 that the meeting took place. I had gone home for weekends a couple of times, but I hadn't had the corrective operation on my windpipe narrowing yet. It can be unusual how key events help to remind you of approximate dates around them. This meant that I couldn't speak at this stage, so my dad did most of the talking from our side of the table because in all honesty I could only acknowledge agreement one way or the other. There was one lawyer who principally ran the meeting and a trainee lawyer was in attendance. Both of them had been investigating our case and its merit.

  They went over details of the case and explained what action we could take. The lawyer in charge asked if I minded discussing the case and looking at photographs. I agreed nonchalantly and at this stage not all the details surrounding the accident had come back to me. It was, however, strange to hear the familiar sounding names of the ski-resort and the town nearby where our accommodation had been, and to see photos of the funicular railway system, the nursery ski-slopes that had been visible out of the apartment window and, in particular, the hut into which I had crashed. This very photograph pictured the hut with snow suspiciously heaped up where the wire fence type protection had been vandalised. Standing next to the hut was a friend, Ellie's dad in fact, and it was dated. The photograph had been taken a couple of days after the accident in order for it to be used as evidence in any legal proceedings that might lie ahead.

It was quite a bizarre feeling to see all this. I almost felt like a bystander or someone hearing this story in a news bulletin. It was as if it was not me who had been the casualty. It all seemed like too much bad luck to be true. Who would believe this whole escapade? While on a toboggan mat, hitting a hut unprotected due to vandalised protection, mother returning to England clutching wire-cutters to free the wires securing the jaw fractures if patient stops breathing, probably paralysed for life, hallucinating on morphine and threatening to throw spears at Zulu nurses, subsequently unable to speak because of a dodgy tracheostomy tube causing windpipe scarring, almost dying of asphyxia before the problem was discovered, and the list goes on. It's so unbelievable, it's almost laughable. Was I dreaming or was this really happening? I often wondered whether I would wake up from this terrible dream. It hasn't happened yet. In this case, the phrase that seemed to ring true was unarguably "when the shit hits the fan….."

There were three choices. First was to do nothing. Second was to pursue a court case. The third choice was a tribunal. The court case would be held in France with me attending to give evidence and it would be more expensive than the tribunal. A tribunal would still have to be conducted in France, but it was cheaper and did not require me to go there. The tribunal seemed the most feasible option. If successful, the way that compensation payment from a tribunal works is to identify an amount that is equivalent to the damages incurred. The solicitors thought that this would be about a million pounds in my case. The person judging the case would then decide what proportion of the accident was the fault of the victim and how much was that of the defendant. The victim gets awarded the proportion of fault attributed to the defendant multiplied by the damage cost identified. So, for example, if it was felt that the accident was 40% my fault and 60% the ski-resort's fault, then I would be awarded 60% of a million pounds.

The case seemed worth proceeding with on a tribunal basis and it was going to cost about £3 000. I was not an irrational accident victim and claiming that it was outrageous that I should be blamed rather than the ski-resort. I could understand that I had gone up the ski-slope with a toboggan mat, when it was dark. I could also see that the ski-resort might argue that the hut had been vandalised just before my accident, leaving little time for them to repair it. I thought it was highly unlikely that this had really happened, but I was sure that the defence would use this line of argument in trying to sway the case in their favour. What was in my favour was the fact that the mats were left at the bottom of the slope for people to use and also the fact that there was easy access to designated slopes after dark. The resort officials also seemed to realise some responsibility on their part for the danger of an unprotected hut after my accident by having packed snow around the hut a day or so later. The resort's culpability was not greatly changed by when the hut protection had been damaged with respect to my accident. After all, had I not had my accident, the vandalism would have probably gone unnoticed for some time. Looking at all the facts, I was willing to take a proportion of the blame, but to take all the blame seemed ludicrous. Even so, not being a lawyer left me in the dark as to how these decisions were made.

We were allowed to consider the different choices and my dad contacted the lawyers a short time after the meeting to say that we would go ahead with the tribunal option. If the tribunal was unsuccessful on the first attempt, we would be allowed one appeal. The tribunal would consist of a brief hearing in which the evidence would be presented, after which a decision would be made on compensation. We had the option to attend the tribunal in France but opted not to do so. It would have only been out of interest to hear what was said there and this would have been a long journey for me. It would have meant more expense, it wouldn't have changed the outcome and they would have been speaking bloody French in any case! It was a matter of waiting to hear the outcome from our solicitors.

My dad was the messenger for me when news of how it had gone filtered back to our lawyers in Bristol. The first tribunal turned out to be unsuccessful. Damn it! Naturally, I felt quite shocked and very disappointed to have been awarded nothing at this hearing. I didn't fly off the handle or anything like that. My dad had a very good way of delivering bad news in a neutral, yet sympathetic, manner. He wouldn't slag off the lawyers until I did and even then he wasn't indiscriminate. He was simply good at empathising. For example, I would mouth or write, "Bloody French, crappy ski-huts, money-grabbing gits, bastards," and other unsavoury language. He would just agree, with a wry smile. He knew that my slagging off session was mainly out of disappointment and frustration, and it was a partly non-serious way to release my emotions. The frustration for all of us in this situation was so very apparent, though. We were still given no compensation, the more frustrated we got.

Now we had to decide on whether to go ahead with a second hearing. My dad and I had another discussion. We felt that it was worth it. It would cost another £2 000 to £3 000. The solicitors said that they could get an eminent lawyer in France to present the case. He was a member of the Bar, in other words a highly trained barrister. This might offer an added thrust to our case. There would be a long wait before the second hearing. It was going to be at least a few months and I had to forget about what had happened and get on with my rehabilitation. Additionally, there were still many operations that lay ahead. I was probably going to need a major operation on my neck, and so I needed to try to gain as much strength as possible in the interim. Good food, plenty of Pick 'n Mix sweet selections to scoff and aerobic exercise was the prescription before further operations. I had to channel my energies into this, instead of being distracted by a silly legal case run by the French.

Chapter 20

Odstock: influential people

As I have alluded already, fellow patients are a source of much strength, encouragement and sanity, believe it or not. It is almost critical to your survival, both mentally and physically, to be part of a community where you can share similar frustrations, give and receive advice, and also have a good laugh. Influence doesn't always have to be positive. It is purely something that shapes you as a person. Don't worry, I won't quote the dictionary definition. So what or who influenced me, other than those mentioned already?

There was one patient, who arrived at the Spinal Injuries Unit about two months after I did. He had sustained a high neck-break, having dived into the shallow part of a swimming pool while on a holiday in Spain. This resulted in tetraplegia and it made him very dependent on people and equipment for survival. He was extremely articulate and projected an air of calmness. His strength of character was evident on speaking to him. There was one occasion, when we were at the stage of being put in wheelchairs. We were both sat in manually propelled wheelchairs by the nurses' station on the ward. I asked him how he was getting on. He said something that struck me, especially since my thoughts had been sensitised as to how important independence was. He said that he had been okay with all that happened to him since his accident, until the other day. It was then that he had been put in a wheelchair for the first time. The chair was not motorised, and so a nurse pushed him to where he wanted to go. He had been left alone for a few minutes, and it was at that moment that he felt completely stranded and utterly helpless. He could not move anywhere, unless he screamed for help. This made me look at myself and think how independent I was, rather than how dependent I was. I couldn't walk or do many of the things that I previously did, but I had not felt such extremes of isolation and total dependence. At the same time, I thought that there were people with more severe impairments than my fellow patient. He was still cerebrally intact and able to attempt to rationalise his situation.

The same person continued to astound me and mould my views. Later on in rehabilitation, he had been supplied with a motorised wheelchair by the ward. I would regularly see him skilfully manoeuvring his chair with a chin control. There was increased independence at last. One evening, however, I saw him back in a manual wheelchair and I asked him why this was so. He told me that a patient, who had a similar chair at home to the forementioned motorised chair, had been admitted for a few days for a minor operation and had been put in the motorised chair because his one at home was being repaired. I asked why he had not asked for it back from this patient, since the chair was officially for him. He said that he could see how much the short stay patient enjoyed the chair. He didn't want to take his enjoyment of freedom away. Selfless, I should say. I fear that not many would do the same. This story could almost be the new definition of the word selfless. What a generous man. Much respect from me. What an honour for me to have had these interchanges and to have known him.

This amazing man who I mention is now back home. He has the equipment that he needs and full-time carers. He is working again in a worthwhile job from home. I would never judge the extent of his disablement; only he can quantify that. Clearly, disability is in the mind of the beholder. Unknowingly, he taught me some important things from his often wise-talking. It certainly made me feel humble, rather than self-pitying, at a time when one can easily end up feeling sorry for oneself. He managed to communicate to me that living with a long-term impairment is idiosyncratic and dynamic. He has much wisdom to give to the average person. He is, indeed, severely able-bodied in mind: just me mocking the use of our language in the realization that someone so severely physically disabled is so wise in mind.

There was another man in his early-twenties who I met when he came back into the Spinal Injuries Unit for supplementary feeding and an operation. He had become very weak and lost a lot of weight while out of hospital. I will not go into great details about his medical problems, which I am sure that he would appreciate. They are not particularly relevant in any case. As a background, though, he had broken his neck in a rugby accident a few years before. This happened shortly before he was to take his A level examinations. It was not ideal timing; as if you plan these things to happen! After all, I don't think any time is a good time to leave yourself paralysed from the neck down. He had some power in his arms and was able to propel a manual wheelchair with his arms and also to drive an adapted car. We got on very well and had long chats. I had not even contemplated driving a car at the time that I met him.

When you encounter someone like this with a higher break than yourself, it gives you hope for and more confidence in your future independence and capabilities. This can be very helpful, when you're in the isolated, almost artificial, hospital environment. It helps you see beyond the sterile white hospital walls. It was good to talk to someone regularly, who had experience of the transition from hospital to community setting. I had met a couple of people, who had already been discharged from hospital, but these had been mainly fleeting encounters. Besides this, it was good for there to be a fellow patient with whom I could go to different parts of the hospital. It made things a lot less boring. It was very therapeutic to slag off together certain people, the hospital and life in an empathic way. Sometimes it could be just to release our emotions about the situations in which we found ourselves. A good "bloody this, bloody that" session could make you feel a lot better, without the need for there to be anything particularly deep and meaningful in what we said. But we were in the position where we could be truly empathetic to one another about many things, because we were both examples of how life could be rotten for no particular reason. We were also coming from a common problem, that of paralysis.

He would ask me questions that would make me think about my situation, too. One that stuck out was, "Have you been in a wheelchair in your dreams yet?" I had not. He had. Would there be a time, when I was in a wheelchair during sleep? Would this be a sign of adjustment or acceptance? The difference between adjustment and acceptance is important here. Since sustaining my injuries, I have been trying to adjust to my situation in any way possible. I would say that I have adjusted well to a new way of living a few years after the accident. This is different from accepting my situation. I don't think that I have fully accepted my situation; accepted that the impairment with which I currently live might not be altered at some time in the future. Even though I go on about not fully accepting my situation, I think that I have accepted it to some extent. After all, I wouldn't risk everything in a desperate attempt for my paralysis to be reversed. Now I would have to weigh up the benefits and risks of anything being done to change my situation. I still have hope for there being some scientific or medical development that might make my impairment change and be easier to live with, but not at all costs. In addition to this, there is a continual development of equipment and society's integration of people with a long-term impairment to make things easier. Fortunately, I can adjust to living a new life, while still not having to accept my situation fully. This thinking has enabled me to get on with my life and at the same time have hope for future change in the back of my mind. It was important for this hope not to overshadow and prevent me trying to tackle the harsh reality of what learning to live with paralysis entailed. Whatever happens in the research side of things, it was indeed fascinating to consider the possibility of wheelchairs appearing in my future dreams and how my attitude to my own situation might develop. Well, I certainly thought so.

    As for other patients that I met along the way, there was a twenty year old girl who had been involved in a car accident. She had broken her back. She was lucky enough to have an incomplete break; in other words, she was a walker. Despite this, she would still need to be in hospital for a few months and her return to walking would be gradual. After initial bed-rest, she would use a wheelchair intermittently for at least a couple of months. She arrived about three months after me and was on the other ward. I would mainly see her down in physiotherapy and we shared the same physiotherapist in Kathy. It was a good common bond because Kathy was such a great person to have as a physio. It was always good to see both Kathy and this female patient in the physio department, as they were both really cheerful and had good senses of humour. Probably a necessity when having to spend protracted periods of time with me! It would put me in a good mood for the day, when meeting people in physio who I found fun and like friends. It even made me want to go to the physio department. It was a more varied day if it could be spent between the ward and physio department. I am still in contact with both of them and we are very good friends. Making these friendships was a really good thing to come out of my accident.

Even when you are a walker, there is a lot of rehabilitation needed initially and even after discharge. It's not just a matter of getting over the initial injuries. Even walkers have to wear body braces to stabilise their spines for a few weeks. There can also be longer-term aspects to think of, which are not always apparent. Chronic pain can be an issue. Also, stamina and back strength has to be developed gradually. This might be further compromised by restrictions on physical activity for a time after the injury. I shouldn't go on about a walker's recovery, as I have not experienced it, and I am consequently not in an ideal position to discuss it. Sadly, I should say. It's here that I have to tell myself: "Less of this wanting to change things, Wellsy; you cannot choose your lot, you cannot turn back time, you're not a walker, so be quiet and move on with your life." Rather than talking about walkers, the main message was that a variety of people met in hospital gave me sanity, strength, enjoyment and lasting friendships. The lasting friendships are very precious.

There was a male walker in his mid-twenties on my ward during my first few months. He left after about four months. He had had an accident while mountain bike scrambling. I didn't know him from Adam and I wouldn't like to judge his previous and present capabilities, or even his accident circumstances. He was generally very pleasant, although a little cocky, and in the main I liked him. That's one reason why the incident that occurred felt so unusual. During the time that he was in hospital, I couldn't speak because of my windpipe problem. One evening he approached me when I was sitting at my bed-space area on the ward. He was being friendly, which I appreciated. Then he went on to talk about my accident, saying that I must have been really drunk. I did not agree with what he was saying because for starters I hadn't been drunk. I had had two drinks on the night of the accident and I was far from being drunk. Even if I had been drunk, it wouldn't have belittled the tragedy and misfortune of what had happened to me. The blatant fact, all the same, was that I was not drunk and here was someone saying, "You must have been really drunk." That sort of comment should only deserve a "Get lost. Don't be so bloody rude and assuming. I wasn't. And what difference would it make anyway? And is it any of your business?" I was there trying to deal with all the misfortune that had happened to me and out of the blue someone was insulting me about it.

My muteness prevented me from cutting in, but it didn't drastically matter because here was someone I hardly knew who was saying these things. He was just a passing acquaintance. He was not someone important in my life. Our lives wouldn't be intertwined for long. Regardless of that, it didn't matter because what's done is done. There was no changing of the past, by dredging it up again or getting annoyed at someone being rude about it. He also said that I was so weak, which was true at that particular moment in time, and that I must have been very weak before everything happened. I think that one of the things he said was, "How come you're so weedy?" The reason I write, "I think," is because I couldn't believe my ears. Was I hearing things? He had been very pleasant until this moment. Initially, I thought that he was just trying to be chummy and clever; but he was now coming across like a spiteful schoolboy bully. What could I say? I hadn't been weak before the accident. My general good fitness had only been to my benefit, although I believe that a lot to do with surviving these kinds of accidents is down to luck. The annoying thing was that I had been probably fitter than he had been, but I was in no fit state to argue the toss. I could not speak to argue back and from now on in our respective lives I would be a lot less physically able. He was a walker. These needless comments came across as being rather smug and certainly were unfounded. I just sat there and took it, with neither acknowledgement nor rising to the bait. What would have been the best answer to his comments? There was little point in trying to answer back. All I should do is always to act differently to how he had acted on this occasion. I had to make the best of me. That was the best way to answer back.

The encounter on that day did teach me a valuable lesson, though. Never should I judge someone's capabilities and circumstances on outward appearances, especially when I do not know them very well. Judge is a good word. You need evidence to make a judgement. A person should be innocent until proved guilty, or capable until proved incapable. He did not know me. I got the impression that he thought me quite a feeble individual. Admittedly, I wasn't keen on doing stunts on mountain bikes like him. Who gives a damn about mountain bike stunts, though? Being cowardly, or sensible in my eyes, about not doing dare devil bike tricks does not make me a weak person. I know that I am determined, and I know that I am also physically and mentally strong. I was just in a situation that made me appear to be weak. It was unnecessary and almost cruel to criticise me, especially at a vulnerable time in my life. The cliché, "Don't judge a book by its cover," rings ever true. My cover looked deceptively damaged at this time of my life and all that I can say is that it's a damn good job that there's a strong and determined centre beneath it.

 Whatever the circumstances of this particular exchange happening, it is without question uncalled for to be critical of someone at any time, when there is nothing to gain for anyone from it. I would be probably unrecognisable to him now that I am independent in voice and capability, as well as five stones heavier now that I'm at my proper weight. I could not defend myself when criticised on that occasion. Also, I could not be bothered: it was far too tiring to communicate when without a voice. I was just listening and learning valuable lessons on how to behave. Maybe he'll read this book and realise his indiscretion. Still, it's all bygones with no lasting malice held. I've got better things to do. "So why write about it?" I hear someone ask. "It's gives an idea of some of what I had to experience, and so it's an important tale to tell," I reply. Don't judge without evidence. Don't judge for no one's benefit. I had better not be my own worst enemy by judging this male patient completely on the one episode mentioned. Everyone makes an occasional mistake. He was wrong in this instance, but I shouldn't go over the top with my overall opinion of him based on this.

 I can imagine that it might be easy, as a walker, to think yourself to be superior to other patients, unless you step back and realise that every patient has their own story and hidden strengths. The female walker, who I mentioned previously, was great. She never expressed judgement. Having got to know her quite well, she has said how lucky she feels she had been. It was interesting to see the contrasting personalities of her and the male walker. Even so, what the male walker said gave me further motivation to succeed. If I got through all this hospital stuff, regained my voice and got the relevant opportunities, I could show him how wrong he was. I don't have any major resentment towards him. Perhaps I should thank him for giving me extra unintentioned motivation. I am now becoming sarcastic in my gratitude. I should resist, what with it being said to be the lowest form of wit. Nonetheless, my enjoyment from it is too strong, so please forgive me.

People can think that the reason that some patients get out of hospital walking and others do not is down to the effort put in. However, this is not true. Virtually everyone down in that physiotherapy gym gives it their all: sweat, pain and tears in some cases. Being a walker or not is mainly down to luck. The basic fact is that the non-walkers have a more badly injured spinal cord than the walkers.

Sustaining an incomplete break, when most function is regained, is virtually a different problem to sustaining a complete break. Everyone who sustains a broken back has the initial anxiety that things will not return to what they were before. The main difference is that those with complete breaks also tend to have profound long-term implications on their functional ability. They have a whole lifetime of worrying about continence issues, accessibility to toilets and other public places, and much more including financial burdens. The incomplete breaks, despite having the possibility of slightly impaired mobility, chronic pain and other problems, have much less of a disruption than those with complete breaks. All people who sustain broken backs will have insights into the horrors of paralysis; it's just that those with complete breaks will be affected a lot more practically.

There were several other patients who influenced me in minor ways. A large variety of incidents had brought them to Odstock. I've mentioned diving into a pool, car crash, mountain bike, rugby and skiing holiday accidents. There was also diving off a pier, an operative complication, horse riding, falling off a toilet and someone who simply woke up paralysed from the neck down. There are lots of cheap jokes that could be made about circumstances, particularly why falling off a toilet might have occurred. But the accidents are no joke and the consequences to the victims are profound. I think something that I took away from all of this was seeing how many people were affected by these twists of fate. Families had to deal with a person who was usually dramatically physically changed. This would often lead to having to either make large alterations to their current house or even move house. Relationships would be strained and in some cases ended. People coped in different ways. You don't often hear the stories of those who don't cope very well for whatever reason. They should not be forgotten. They are the people who maybe should be offered most help or from whom we can learn the most about ways to help. Sometimes, though, it is being given time and lots of it, rather than help, which soothes the wounds, often emotional ones.

Some patients would have occasional tantrums. There were a couple notorious for this when I was there. One of these infamous individuals would start chucking things and striking out at people from his bed. On one occasion, for some reason he was moved hurriedly on his bed to the eight-bedded area of the ward in the middle of one of his psycho attacks. I can remember looking on to see him hit out at any staff member who dared to approach his bed. This patient had a suprapubic urinary catheter in place to manage his bladder. This is a tube which goes through the lower abdominal wall and into the bladder. It is connected to a urine collection bag at one end. At the other end, it is secured in the bladder with an inflatable balloon. To my dismay, he grabbed the tube and started pulling at it angrily back and forth. The tube stretched and stretched under the tension. I could not believe what he was doing. He was treating his body with such disregard. I had to look away, so did not see the full horror of the damage caused. This made me think that, no matter how low I got, I was probably handling my situation better than some.

I can remember another time when another patient, known for his frequent tantrums, was telling people where to go in pretty unpleasant language from his bed. He certainly wasn't giving directions to the hospital canteen! A charge nurse told him to be quiet. The patient chucked an empty plastic bottle at him. The charge nurse rather stupidly threw it back angrily. This wasn't wise: it was like lighting the touch paper to a piece of dynamite. I was sharing a four-bedded area with the patient at this time. My brother Ali was sitting with me at my bed-space. This patient started chucking anything near his bed on the floor. The charge nurse again returned and pulled the curtains around the patient's bed to enclose him away from others. Then, objects started coming over the top of the curtains. It was hilarious in a rather perverse way but my brother, ever the sensible one, indicated that we should go somewhere else, lest a hard object landed on our heads. What entertainment! Seen in the right context, in other words if you knew the people involved, it was really quite funny. I must admit that secretly I was on the patient's side because I could see how frustrated and angry he was with everything that had happened.

Despite his occasional outcries and going on about how hard he was, he was actually an okay bloke. That's the patient, and not my brother, although my brother is an okay bloke nonetheless. This patient was never unpleasant to me and probably being able to reflect openly on his toughness was his way of coping with his situation. It must be very difficult to go from being very strong, with it perhaps being one of your defining features, to having a high neck-break and being dependent on others. This patient had been in the army, so his fitness had been very important to him. It is bad for anyone to be struck down with paralysis, but from some a similar injury can appear to take away more from some than from others. I guess that every life event has a different context for different people, dependent on their background.

This patient needed a sense of humour as well, though, when my mum gave him some sweets as he lay in bed. My brother had bought them in Belgium and they were truly disgusting. They should have been joke sweets. I could have marketed them as vomit joke sweets: "Taste like vomit, make you vomit, sweets for your enemies." I guess they could have been marketed in this way already, as we couldn't translate the labeling on the packet. After she had put two in his mouth, I saw what she had done and told her how "gross" they were. When she asked him what they tasted like, he politely said that he didn't want to be rude and spit them out, but that he had tasted better. Even the tantrum people have some politeness and can also be quite funny.

The same patient was also renowned for comments that he would make when hanging around at the nurses' desk. One of his comments related to quite an upper-crust father of one the patients, who would often visit. He was a bit of a ya ya, lovely to see you person, who seemed pleasant and certainly wasn't offensive. The only thing was that he stuck out a bit among the congregation of lesser social classes than his. The patient would see him coming and say to everyone else under his breath, "Oh, bloody hell, here comes the posh f*cker!" It's just as well that not all things are heard by everyone. It did amuse us, though. I think that most people sniggered, in response to his comment, more out of shock than anything. The same patient was a bit obnoxious to another patient and his wife, when they asked him to turn down the volume of his music. The wife was infuriated a day or so later, after what had happened had sunk in. She swore that she would kick him in the crotch if he did it again. My parents and I kept a straight face when she told us this. We laughed a lot later, nicknaming her "crotch kicker" in our family group, and further reflected that he wouldn't feel the kick all the same.

    A patient, who had been discharged from hospital a few years before, visited me. This was when I was at an early stage of my hospital stay. I was in the eight-bedded part of the ward and I had not met him previously. The reason he saw me was because he was a medical student when he had his accident, so I guess that we had a few things in common. I seem to remember that he had been involved in a rugby accident, resulting in a neck-break. He had finished his medical training after his accident. He had limited upper limb movement and he had managed to get through the exams by having someone to write for him in them and to do physical examination of patients at his instruction. I might not have the exact details correct of how he had achieved his medical degree. He had done it, though, and he had had a higher spinal cord injury than me. I suppose that his visit had been to show me that there is life after spinal cord injury. His wife and children accompanied him. He had had the children since his accident. He did not stay long and I wasn't particularly vocal, tracheal stricture and all. At that stage of my hospital stay, I was more intent on survival. Having a fulfilling life seemed a distant prospect. It seemed a real improbability to me at the time. It's amazing how you progress, and how your goals and outlook on life change. Role models or, as I'd rather phrase it, people living a valuable life can be powerful motivators.

    The nurses were fantastic. They had to put up with a lot of hassle from patients and despite this they were very supportive and also really good fun. There was a duo who would almost always be on the same shift. "What are you like?" would often ring out in a local accent, when I was being particularly stupid or lazy. They were so funny. We used to tease each other about different things, but it was all good-natured. Then there was another nurse in her mid-twenties, who would always be smiling and really helpful. She would go and make me a cuppa secretly, sometimes when a senior nurse was telling me that I had to go to do it myself. There were plenty of other really friendly nurses. It was in many ways like a hospital social club, even though us patients were working hard to be ready to leave. When the nurses that I got on with really well were working, it made the day better. It was someone else to talk to. In all honesty, I probably got to know a lot of the staff better than many of the patients.

There were also many visitors. There was a fine line between seeing all the people who had made the effort to visit and resting my traumatised body. It was good to see people, though, and lots of relatives and friends came. My mum's brother and some of my cousins lived near to Salisbury and one of them is a nurse who had worked at the Spinal Injuries Unit previously. Hence she was obviously familiar with the routine of spinal cord injury rehabilitation, although I'm sure that she didn't wish to be returning as a visitor. It was really strengthening to have all this support and people just coming to see me was all that was needed. It was easier if the visitors made the conversation in most cases, rather than me struggling. I felt privileged to have so many people willing to make time to visit. It was appreciated beyond words, but still that doesn't mean that I should not say it. Let me say thanks now: thank you indeed. It's a lot later, but that does not negate its sincerity.

There were times when the other patients, as well as myself, were vulnerable. This can enlighten you to aspects of people's personality that you might not see in ordinary circumstances. Somehow we were all in extraordinary situations, which made the time in hospital truly unique. Each person was trying to cope with his or her situation, and so would naturally have visible scars. No matter how much I thought that I had discovered about someone, I still didn't fully know them. I didn't know what exactly lay beneath their outward shell, under their outward appearance, behind their curtains. This was very apparent to me, especially since for a lot of my time I couldn't speak which meant that a lot about me was hidden from others. Idle chit chat didn't have the chance to dominate my interactions with people. Some people, fortunately not many, would say some inappropriate comments and I couldn't correct them succinctly with a swift, and preferably enlightening, vocal response. At times, it was very frustrating to endure. There was so much behind my outward appearance.

    I remember an incident that particularly annoyed me. It was when someone mockingly imitated my efforts to squeeze air past my vocal cords in attempts to force a voice. It only happened the once and the guilty party will remain nameless. Disbelief entered my head, alongside other unpleasant emotions. Perhaps the person just didn't think about what they were doing. I didn't want to waste the time and effort in trying to answer them back. Answer back, who's kidding who? That really is taking the Michael. In any case, this person was just a momentary passer-through during that period of my life. I just forced a smile thinking to myself, "Shut up, you rude person. Put yourself in my position, and be a little more pleasant and adept in approaching me. You're not funny. If you can't think of anything to say that isn't obnoxious, please just be quiet." I can think of more choice words than that; but would they be worth it? There's only so much time and energy that one has to do purposeful things in this life, so it was best to let it lie. Best to move on rather than getting over-annoyed and obsessive about other people's momentary indiscretions. Incidents like this were made tolerable by having fantastic key people around me, who were brilliant in their attitudes and behaviour. It was how I was considered by the people close to me that mattered. There were no demeaning or judgemental comments from them.

    Everyone who mattered was great. The ones that don't matter, literally don't matter. I'd soon dismiss to one side the ignorant comments or behaviour of people not close to me. If somebody makes a stupid comment, it reflects more on their inadequacies than on my situation. I need to appreciate that people might feel uncomfortable when interacting with someone with an obvious physical impairment, as well as the fact that some people just see the surface and not the whole. That's why the reason for a stupid comment isn't always as obvious or as badly intentioned as it might appear. Years on, I have much hidden inside me, as most people do. Everyone wants their own personal space after all, and so is bound to have secrets. There is a very useful lesson in life from all this. I keep repeating it because it is so very important: never judge someone completely on his or her outward appearance. Equally, never judge anyone for one stupid comment. You don't know what goes on deep inside a person. Treat people with respect. Treat people as you would like to be treated.

Chapter 21

Assessment for tracheal reconstruction

It was November 1992 when the London ear, nose and throat surgeon visited me for the second time. The first time had been a few months before. It had been an initial assessment under general anaesthetic, when the site of narrowing had been inspected and a dilatation of the area attempted. He found out, at that operation, that the windpipe narrowing was sufficiently low enough below the vocal cords to allow a major corrective surgical procedure, if needed. He had decided to wait a few months to see if the scarring in my windpipe would decrease adequately to make surgery unnecessary.

I had had a very frustrating time with communication up to this point. My communication methods ranged from writing things down to mouthing words to belching out noises, so-called oesophageal speech. This oesophageal speech may sound like it's pretty disgusting, but it was a great relief when I found a way to produce some sort of vaguely comprehensible sound. It was still not fluent speech and only a few people could understand me. Nonetheless, it was at least a release from total muteness. In the main, though, it was far easier to write things down to communicate or simply to move my head in a nod or shake motion in response to yes-no type questions and comments. I tried to do whatever used up the least amount of energy. It had been a long time to endure this terrible frustration. Even so, the lack of speech had given me the opportunity to be thoughtful and inward-looking in a good and almost therapeutic manner. I didn't have to bother with small talk. It was such an effort to communicate that often I would be left alone, rather than having to force a chatty conversation. I learned a lot about myself and gained confidence in not having to say something for embarrassment's sake.

At last, the time had come for the surgeon's reassessment of my throat. My hope was for a glint of progress with my communication difficulty. He was a very busy man and arrived at about eleven o'clock at night. He was encouraged by the fact that now I could produce some sounds, even though not particularly comprehensible. I was currently in one of the four-bedded sections of the ward, a promotion from the eight-bedded section. I was told to lie flat on the bed with just one pillow beneath my head to have my neck in the optimum position for inspection. On this occasion, he was going to assess the windpipe narrowing with a flexible telescope through my tracheostomy hole while I was awake on the ward. Now was the time that I hated, which was when the tracheostomy tube was removed. There was a feeling of security in having the tracheostomy tube firmly taped in place by neck straps either side of it. This was especially the case because the hole in my neck was my sole airway, due to my windpipe above the tube being profoundly narrowed. Hence, every time the tracheostomy tube was taken out, I would be motionless, helpless and very dependent on the operator performing the procedure. This surgeon gave an air of confidence and was able to put me at ease, even when things might not be straightforward. In any case I should not have been nervous because this was a routine check on how things were going.

      The straps were removed carefully. If removed without stabilising the tube, it could be uncomfortable and cause me to splutter. Next, out came the tube. These procedures rely on eye contact and simple head movements for communication with the operator. It was pointless trying to speak, since sounds would not be produced and it might project unwanted secretions into the area of the tracheosteomy hole. He had a look in through the hole in my neck using the flexible telescope type of equipment that he brought with him. He said that it was still a little tight but a slight improvement from earlier in the year. He mentioned that he might be able to avoid a major operation. By this, I think that lasering alone might have been an option. He went away briefly to fashion a new tracheostomy tube to reinsert.

      On his return, he reassessed the situation. The situation had now become a bit more difficult than a short moment ago. A small bit of cartilage in my windpipe wall was loose near the tracheostomy hole in my neck and there was some bleeding occurring into my windpipe. This was a very tricky scenario. He had a closer look and explained that the light in the ward was not bright enough for him to put the tube back in. He got a suction catheter, readily available at my bedside and usually used for clearing secretions from the tracheostomy tube. He cut the catheter midway along its length making it shorter and then placed it through my tracheostomy hole. He told me what was happening and explained what I needed to do. I was to keep my eyes open at all times, stay calm and to try to breathe through both the narrow gauge suction catheter placed in the hole in my neck and my very narrow windpipe above. These two narrow breathing apertures would not be able to sustain me for long. The reason for keeping my eyes open was to show that I was still conscious and not deteriorating. By now, many nurses were around the bed helping out. The on-call anaesthetist was called to the ward as an emergency. I was totally reliant on the calmness of the surgeon and the efficiency of the nurses, as much as they were on me. If I panicked, the outcome could be fatal. This was true doctor-patient partnership. Every so often, suctioning of blood with the catheter would be performed and the catheter changed. I started to shiver. I don't know why. It just happened and despite this I was still very conscious and alert to the seriousness of the events and I was not going to relax my concentration. When the anaesthetist arrived, my bed was hurriedly wheeled up the corridor. My bed, two nurses, and the surgeon and anaesthetist travelled the long three hundred yards to theatres. It was to be another unplanned operation.

 A needle prick was felt as the line to administer the anaesthetic went into one of my arm veins when in theatre. Immediately after this, I had the anaesthetic injected into my bloodstream. I began to feel lightheaded and could feel myself drifting off. It was such a relief to be put to sleep. Whatever happened now, I was away from this stressful situation. Everyone had been superb. The nursing staff, who can often be unappreciated, had been paramount in keeping the problem contained. Yet again, I owe thanks to wonderful people.

 My next memory is waking up on the ward. The surgeon approached me. By this time, it was about six in the morning. He apologised, saying that this sort of thing happened very rarely. I think that he said once in ten years from his own experience. There was a lot of mutual respect for each other, having both been through a very tricky time just a few hours previously when we were totally reliant on one another's calmness. I reciprocated that things had been unfortunate, knowing that his visit had been prolonged by this inconvenient slip of cartilage. I think that he realised that I had been a dead ringer for bad luck in the last few months and was as a consequence used to these inconveniences. There was almost a common understanding of life's unpredictability and indiscriminateness in dishing out stressful situations. Having seen how my breathing had been during this episode, he now felt that he needed to operate. This would be planned for two weeks' time. He was very generous in offering to come to Salisbury to do the operation with the consultant surgeon from Salisbury. They had worked together previously and proved to make a good team.

  This support makes you feel optimistic and forward-looking when you are treated in what seems like, and what probably is, a special manner. At a time when you cannot speak, walk, control your bowels and bladder conventionally, and you are trying to rationalise things, every glimpse of kindness and hope goes a long way. Hope is the key. You do not know how much you can cope with until you are in the situation. What can be said is that you can surprise yourself by what you can achieve, and support can often carry you through the challenges. Hope can be anything from being able simply to talk with someone, to wanting to be a first-class academic, to being able to get out of bed rather than be shackled to it by immobility. It is variable both between individuals and in the same individual with time. After all, my main hopes now are different from those that I had soon after my accident. I do, however, value independence more than I did before my accident and a new perspective on life has been gained, whatever my future goals might be. I know what it is like to be very dependent and I appreciate the functional autonomy that I now have.

  The London surgeon had many aspects to his background which made him somehow an ideal choice to do my throat surgery. His surgical skill is without question. He would see a problem and approach it sensibly and not over-elaborately. Also, I'm pretty sure that he is a pioneer in his field and that there couldn't have been a person better equipped for tackling my windpipe problem. I found out years later, from a newspaper cutting my brother Ali found, that I was amongst illustrious company as one of his patients. He had performed surgery on the famous scientist Stephen Hawking to prevent him aspirating food and drink, despite other colleagues warning of the difficulty of the operation. I read that, without the operation, Stephen

Hawking would have almost certainly died. See a problem and fix it seemed to be his practice, and it seemed to work. In addition to this, the throat surgeon had broken his back some twenty years previously, after falling down a couple of steps while in a hurry. He had needed to lie flat in bed for a month or two following this. Fortunately for him, and also me, there had been no permanent injury to his spinal cord. He was extremely easy to get on with, too. The nurses raved about how good he had been that night and he acknowledged how invaluable they had been during the turn of events with the slipped bit of cartilage by writing so in the medical notes. All people involved that night were recognised rightly for their praise-deserving attributes.

Many patients present on the ward at the time of the night's excitement were concerned for my welfare. The disruptions during the night had not gone unnoticed by the three female patients with whom I been sharing a four-bedded section of the ward. I was one of the ladies by inference, if you want to be cheeky. In such circumstances, did I give a damn what I was called? I was simply a bloke in a desperate situation trying to beat it. I couldn't care less what people called me.

So who were these concerned fellow patients? One was an elderly lady from Barnstaple. She had had one of her legs fused at the knee when young. Following a spinal cord injury, she was now in a wheelchair with one leg extended as she couldn't bend it at the knee. Quite a distinctive look and an added difficulty to mobility. She was great fun……Devonshire accent and all. She would speak her mind. Once she was dressing on her bed behind the surrounding curtains and a young doctor popped his head around the curtains and said, "Don't worry, I'm a doctor." Back came the female patient's reply, "I don't give a damn who you are. You're a man, so get out of here." She was funny. She liked Victor Meldrew in the One Foot in the Grave television programme. Reflecting on her, she was in some ways like a female Victor Meldrew: she spoke her mind, had a good sense of humour and was funny. I like Victor Meldrew. Cheers fellow patient, it was fun knowing you.

The other two ladies in the four-bedded area were likewise easy to get on with. There were only two criticisms. Well, they're not really criticisms. Let's call them observations or incidents. One of the ladies would go on and on about men and how unreliable they were. I would sit quietly in the corner, as she would complain about them. She may have had good reasons, but I didn't particularly want to find out. Best not get involved. "Don't go there, boy!" as they say on American chat shows. I was happier in the distant listener role. The other thing happened when I was on a shower chair over one of the toilets in the Spinal Injuries Unit. The door opened, as I was perched there. I had stupidly not locked it. It was one of the ladies and there was a crowd of about five patients a few feet behind her. They all cracked up in a chorus of laughter. She, of course, didn't know that I would be there and though I looked shocked, she did even more so. She felt really guilty but we all eventually saw the funny side. It was certainly memorable. These stories have little to do with the windpipe assessment other than to communicate how there was a community spirit among the patients on the ward. If things happened to fellow patients, there would be interest and concern from the others and this concern had been very apparent in the case of my midnight trip to the operating theatre. Comradeship goes a long way to helping your mood and approach to life: very important in the early stages of recovery from the situations in which we spinal cord injury patients found ourselves. I had fortunately survived yet another adventure and that had been apparent to everyone.

Chapter 22

Tracheal reconstruction

It was 6 December 1992. The morning of the tracheal reconstruction operation had arrived. I had been allowed a very early light-breakfast of a couple of pieces of toast because the operation was in the early afternoon. My mum arrived at around about ten that morning and she was here for the day. It was a pretty major operation in that it was very technical and involved operating on a fairly vital structure. After all, you cannot really mess around willy-nilly with your windpipe.

  It had not been a very difficult decision as to whether or not to proceed. I needed my voice back to live a more independent life. I also wanted to get rid of the very annoying and literally tiresome tracheostomy tube at some stage. A tricky operation was well worth the gamble. I had also grown to have much faith in the surgeons and although that didn't mean that it would go right it certainly gave me added confidence to approach the procedure with less fear. It had not instilled false optimism and I felt that I had reached a realistic level of understanding concerning the benefits and risks of surgery. I had been told that the main operation with follow-up lasering operations had an eighty percent success rate. I might be one of the unlucky one in five who couldn't be cured of this problem but I didn't dwell on this. The best thing, I felt, was to get on with it and see where I ended up next. I considered myself to be in the best hands for this undertaking, thanks to my family's and friends' homework on the subject. All I could do now was to let the experts take over. It must have been yet another hard day for friends and family, having me go through another life event and maybe even having to hope that it wouldn't be a death event.

  It was good to have my mum's calm company for the morning. It was a stressful day for everyone, but my mum and I didn't discuss what was going to happen in great detail. We were just supportive of each other, but not in a sickeningly outward or hysterical manner. My mum was supportive by just being there. Also, we had had plenty of time to get used to very few words being spoken, particularly on my part. There was the feeling of knowing that we were in this together. Whatever happened in the day ahead, we had one another's support and willing. More of the family were coming later in the day.

The theatre porters came to take me up for the operation. I waved goodbye to my mum and the trolley was wheeled in the direction of the theatre, a not unfamiliar journey for me. At least this time the operation was planned. The anaesthetist put a cannula into one of my arm veins once in the anaesthetic room. Before I felt the warm, drowsy and pleasant sensation in my head of the general anaesthetic injection taking effect, the two surgeons entered the room. Both of them greeted me cheerfully with welcoming smiles. The London surgeon asked if I was okay and briefly explained that he would have to leave soon after the surgery. The Salisbury surgeon, who he knew from before, would be around in the hospital that day for some time after the operation to see how I was recovering. I gave nods and smiles of acknowledgement and also relief to be having an operation on my throat at last. It had been worth the wait of a few months to see if things had improved on their own, as the operation was no light undertaking. Impatience and rushing into unnecessary surgery was a fool's game. However, it was good to be now finally at the stage where my absence of voice could be rectified. Rather than worry, I was raring to get on with it.

My next memory was of being back on the ward, gradually regaining consciousness. The state from anaesthesia to consciousness is quite a queer feeling. You feel yourself go through varying levels of consciousness. I can remember initially opening my eyes and seeing my mum reading a novel at my bedside. At this stage, all I could do was observe. Then I caught my mum's eyes. They are a pure blue colour and full of vitality and caring. Even the white bits of her eyes have a hue of blue. Soon I'll be a poet, and don't I know it! A smile was exchanged between the two of us. She then carried on reading. She could obviously tell that I was not yet in a state to do anything else. She must have been relieved that I had been returned to the ward safely and was now slowly waking up from the anaesthetic. Her presence there was very strengthening for me. She was indeed someone who I could truly rely on being there for me in times of trouble. As I became more awake, I mustered a "hello." My voice had returned and it was no longer an effort to communicate freely. It seemed almost magical being able to open my mouth and for words to come out. It's amazing how such an everyday capability is taken for granted until it is lost. Now that my ability to speak had been regained, I knew that I would never take it for granted again.

    I had a tight device around my neck. This was a hard compression bandage, which was essentially necessary to help hold my neck together. I attempted to drink some liquid but this was quite difficult due to the compression bandage's pressure on my throat. Spasms can get worse when the person feels off colour, for whatever reason. My legs were quite jumpy following the main operation. Spasms were indeed abounding in them. Muscle spasms, involuntary movement of parts of the body below the level of spinal cord injury, can occur when spinal cord injury is permanent for someone. There is medicine that can be taken to lessen the severity of the spasms and I tried to swallow some of this medicine, a baclofen tablet, to achieve this. Tablets were a no-no and liquid baclofen was fetched as an alternative. The spasms were tolerable and the baclofen might have made the leg spasms slightly more bearable but it wasn't essential for me to get it into me. What really mattered was how the surgery had gone.

    The Salisbury surgeon came on the ward to see how I was. He reassured me that the swallowing difficulty was due to the tight collar and that my swallowing would return to normal when the collar could be removed in a couple days. He said that things had gone well. This was as much to reassure my mum as me, which was important. I had to take antibiotics for six weeks as a safeguard against the operation site becoming infected. An infection at the operation site would be bad news. I was also not allowed to strain my neck for a similar duration. This was because a small neck muscle had been stitched to the front of my windpipe to hold it together where it had been opened to perform the surgery.

    It had been quite a procedure. I hope that I have got the general details of surgery correct. My windpipe had been cut lengthways. The scar tissue had been cut out of the inside of it. Some skin had been taken from my left thigh and this skin had been used to line my windpipe where the scar tissue had been removed. A plastic hollow tube of a couple of centimeters in length, shaped rather like a hula hoop crisp and also known as a stent, was then placed on the inside of the windpipe over the operated area. The front of the windpipe had next been stitched back together with part of a neck muscle attached across the area for support. A new tracheostomy tube was in place slightly lower in my neck than before. I think that this was because it enabled the surgery on the higher bit of windpipe to be performed more easily. It also meant that I still had an alternative airway to my normal windpipe after the operation.

The limitation of not straining my neck for six weeks meant that I was not allowed to transfer myself from wheelchair to bed on my own. I would have to be lifted using a hoist. More on that later. The surgeon left having seen that no problems had occurred. This was unusual for me based on past performance. Performance is a good word here, as there had been quite a few dramas. The surgeon was aware of this and that I might be a bit of a jinx from my track record so far, so I'm pretty sure that he was pleased to see nothing untoward had occurred yet. More of the family arrived that day. They could see that I was tired and they left after they saw that I was in safe hands for the rest of the day. I exchanged a few words effortlessly for the first time in what had seemed like an eternity. I was not guaranteed long-term success from the operation. There was a chance that the operated area might become scarred again and occlude the windpipe which meant that operations every three months lay ahead of me to examine this area under general anaesthetic using a telescope device. The idea was to laser any areas of scar tissue that looked immature or occlusive of the windpipe aperture. The tracheostomy tube could only be removed when the inside of the windpipe looked wide and mature enough.

The next visit from the London surgeon was planned for early February. The prospect of getting rid of the tracheostomy tube at that stage seemed a distant thing. "Take one thing at a time, be patient, don't jump the gun or you'll fall down hard, be thankful for the progress so far, be grateful that you can now speak rather than obsessively thinking about the tracheostomy tube," I had to keep reminding myself. After all, removal of the tracheostomy tube wasn't guaranteed at the next operation. In fact permanent success from the initial surgery wasn't guaranteed because the scar tissue could regrow and I could be back where I was in before the initial operation, namely unable to speak freely. I had to try to live in the present as much as possible. Being given the ability to speak again was truly amazing for me. Although I was exceptionally grateful to be able to speak again and I appreciated that being able to speak was far more important than getting rid of the tracheostomy tube, it was hard not to be impatient because tracheostomy tubes can be so intolerable.

Chapter 23

Vocal at last and hoisted by nurses

It was great to chat spontaneously. The nurses were generally a fantastic group of people and now they could get to know my personality even more. Poor them! I bet they had some comments for the throat surgeon. "Now that you've done this surgery, we've got to put up with this bloke's verbal abuse." In all seriousness, it did make things a lot easier for me. I had to be hoisted into bed, though, but this was a very small price to pay. Being hoisted was a rather strange feeling. A harness device would be attached to me and this was then attached to a hoisting machine. I would be hoisted in the air with a winch device on the hoist and then the machine was moved to where I needed to be deposited, usually the bed or chair. When being carried in the hoist machine, I did feel quite unsteady and certainly out of control. I had to trust the operators, usually a nurse or therapist.

The hoisting process took quite a lot of time, so I wasn't able to get out of my chair on to the bed much during the day. Although this meant that a midday nap was more difficult to arrange, I didn't have to do any physiotherapy to tire me. No neck stretching, you see. Even though I joke about not having to do exertion as being an easy life, it would have been better to keep my learned skills from rehabilitation going rather than taking a step back or perhaps sideways. There were a couple of things delaying my hospital discharge. The throat problem was one and not having a suitable place to live was another. I wasn't unique in needing to find a place to live. It was going to be some time before the proposed renovation of the derelict cottage bought by my parents would be completed. I was therefore not in a great rush to leave hospital. Had I been, the delay resulting from the throat surgery would have been very frustrating.

I had reached a stage when most of my hospital rehabilitation was finished and I was now having to take things easy for a few weeks. It was so good to speak again. All that terrible frustration with communication was over. Nonetheless, I did still get tired. The tracheostomy tube in itself made me weary. I had to suction secretions from it often and there was still anxiety held by me over how delicate the neck area was. The tube had an additional thin tube, which hung to the side of it. It was a few centimeters long and its purpose was to inflate with air a cuff that surrounded the lower part of the tracheostomy tube. I was very conscious of people coming near my neck because of the tracheostomy and accompanying thin tube. I worried that if anyone yanked that thin tube by mistake, the tracheostomy tube itself would be pulled out of my neck. An accident waiting to happen, I thought. Hence, I wouldn't let anyone take my tops off when I dressed. Only I could do it, lest the thin tube was tugged.

      One evening, just a few days before Christmas, I had just been hoisted on to my bed. One of the nurses went to do what had been worrying me. The accident waiting to happen did in fact happen. She grabbed at my top to pull it off and with it pulled the thin tube and out came the tracheostomy tube. She saw what she had done. Both of us froze in disbelief, horror apparent in our faces. After this momentary freeze frame, realisation took effect and she rushed to get the sister who in turn got the ward doctor. No one wanted to risk replacing the tube, as it lay dangling from my neck with a gaping tracheostomy hole apparent. The Salisbury throat surgeon was contacted as a matter of urgency. He arrived within a few minutes, which was very impressive for an evening's unplanned visit. We exchanged friendly smiles and familiar looks of, "here's another fine mess we've got ourselves into." Laurel and Hardy, here we come! Well, it was really more like, "here we go again; life isn't dealing us good cards; how long can this go on?" At least no general anaesthetic was needed this time. He put in a new tracheostomy tube on the ward and cut off the dangling external thin tube, saying that we didn't need it or want the same thing to happen again.

      The nurse who did the pulling was distraught by what she had done and although I was initially a bit annoyed that she had grabbed for my top, she was certainly not going to do it again and I could see how upset she was. She hadn't done it deliberately and the incident was soon passed over by me, although not completely forgotten. I had no lasting ill effects from what had happened and it had simply been an accident. Move on, don't dwell, look on the bright side, worry about the important things ahead and consider the whole picture. It was just another episode in my catalogue of adventures. In fact, not long after, the nurse involved and I managed to share a smile of amusement about how shocked we had both looked.

Chapter 24

December 1992: a hospital Christmas

One of the best Christmases ever! Am I mad? Paraplegic, pain, hospital food, away from home and fully institutionalised. There was, however, the following: family, friends, recently regained ability to speak, presents from friends not normally always seen and new friends among the staff and fellow patients. I felt valued more than usual and appreciated this very much. Most importantly, though, I valued friends, family and life more than ever. I also valued my ability to communicate more easily with friends, now that my voice was here at last. Every day and every good friendship was special and these were gifts more special than anything money could buy. My good friendships had truly been enriched.

Life had almost been taken away from me on more than one occasion. It had not been taken away, though, and I was able to enjoy life and its riches now, these being all the better from the perspective of someone who felt lucky to be still alive. I could still taste the highs and lows of life knowing that it could have been so easily different. When you feel privileged to be still alive and able to have the highs and lows of life, you seem to be able take the lows so much more in your stride, certainly able to take them more philosophically. You are simply grateful to be experiencing life. Well, that's at least been my experience. I even value the lows knowing how they add to the variety and make the highs taste sweeter.

Did I deserve to be still alive? Certainly I appreciate that I had been so very lucky to survive and I expect that there have been many unlucky ones before me who died when in similar circumstances to mine. They had not been given a second chance at life. And chance is the right word. It's like rolling dice. The dice that I rolled probably had thousands of sides and only one of the sides was survival; one in a million more like. All I can say is that I am very lucky to be here and that I had better make the most out of the cards dealt my way. I tell myself, "Don't squander your chance at life like some ungrateful idiot, Wellsy. Give a bit back, too. It had better not be take, take,

take. You have a privileged and powerful position to influence many people if you make a success out of your life from now on." But what is success in any case? That's another chapter in itself.

I have strayed from a chapter on Christmas cheer. Certainly, I hoped to take, take, take lots of presents, even though my philosophy on life from this time forward was for me to do a bit of giving. Despite my many obvious external scars of a young life interrupted, I felt that my life had already shown me more than most others experience in their whole lives. I was here to continue my eventful life story. It was truly inspirational to have my family share Christmas Day and Boxing Day with me. We were still all here together. I opened some presents and I had little for them in return, other than my presence and gratitude. Lunch was served in the dining area, which made a pleasant change from the ward. The consultant doctors carved the turkey and there were six tables, each sitting a patient and his or her respective party of friends and family. Tasty food, crackers, paper hats, cracker jokes and a glass of wine were the ingredients to the meal. It was a good day and even though it was in hospital it was a relaxing atmosphere and the focus was on enjoyment. There was no threat of physiotherapy or other hospital rehabilitation. Boxing Day was a little more low key and my family came down again. I wasn't given the chance to feel lonely, which could be easily downhearting at a time such as Christmas. All cheers, no sneers.

Loads of friends came down on the 27th. What an uplift it was. I had hundreds of presents to open, too. There was nothing that I wanted in particular and the presents were mainly bric-a-brac. It was the ability to receive presents in the company of friends, almost like old times away from the hospital, that made this day feel so good. When you have many of your liberties taken away by injuries and circumstances, you simply value regaining some of the freedom which used to be taken for granted. Real life was returning: it was now defeating the incarcerating hospital life forced upon me a few months before. I felt very lucky to have so many people who cared so much. Excited thank yous were said on opening presents. It was a brilliant feeling to have such company. It was everyone's presence and generosity of spirit that mattered to me and it was there in abundance. This was not, however, a sycophantic affair. It was simply people enjoying each other's company.

I would be stupid and lying, though, if I didn't admit to liking the presents, too. Who wouldn't want about twenty friends hand over presents to them constantly? Breaking one's back and almost dying on a few occasions, however, is not a recommended way to achieve this. It was fantastic to be celebrating for a change. Christmas was for enjoyment. Enjoy the present….and the presents! It was just such a pleasure to have so many people there who had gone out of their way to visit me. It was very touching and despite my newly found speaking ability I couldn't vocalise my feelings adequately. I reflect on the events with fondness and appreciate them greatly. Even so, I would need to be there again to capture them properly. With time, things are forgotten in their entirety. I have not forgotten, though, how valuable friends and family are. They should never be taken for granted. What a wonderful group of people, truly stars in my life. "Now he is getting sycophantic," I hear people mutter. But you had to be there and you have to be me, to know that it's a sincere reflection. Stars in my life: that almost sounds like a terrible television talent show or some reunion show. The vocabulary used doesn't matter. It's the sentiments rather than the words that are important.

Chapter 25

The wrong tube or the wrong neck?

There were two different types of tracheostomy tubes stocked at the hospital. I had been going on at one of the more senior nurses about how my current tube kept on migrating out of my neck. I explained that I didn't have this problem when I had had the other make of tube. Until I got fitted with one of these tubes, I had to keep nudging the current tube back in place lest it fall out. It was very frustrating because I got the impression that the forementioned nurse didn't appreciate my concern and urgency to get the current one replaced. Some patients might think that they are the most important and deserving and unreasonably want things done quickly. I don't think that I had been unreasonable in my request for a more suitable tracheostomy tube. Even if it had been an unreasonable urgent request, it had been made repeatedly by me over a long period of time. Reflecting on what happened in this instant, maybe I should have been more assertive and less polite with my request.

At least I had had the major corrective surgery on my windpipe and did not rely on the tracheostomy tube for my main source of breathing. I had been putting a red bung on the end of the tube throughout the day, so that I was solely using my normal airway for breathing. The reason for me having the tube still in place was because after the most recent operation the scarring was immature. In other words, there was still a chance that the scar tissue at the operation site could proliferate and occlude my windpipe. The tracheostomy tube meant that I had a safeguard alternative airway to my natural windpipe if this happened.

I was at home for a weekend. The tube had been coming out a bit as usual. I had been constantly pushing it back into my neck. My breathing had not been a problem, which made me less concerned. As the weekend went on, I felt that I was unable to reposition it fully in its original position. The tube felt as if it had migrated quite a distance out of my neck. My dad drove me back to the Spinal Injuries Unit on Sunday afternoon. We mentioned the problem, when we arrived. The doctor on the ward had a look. Having assessed me, he felt that the Salisbury consultant surgeon, present at the major throat reconstruction procedure, should be called. Within twenty minutes, the consultant surgeon arrived with his registrar. He had the necessary equipment to check me out properly. Indeed, he confirmed my fears that the tube had come out quite some way. The tissues of my neck had closed over and were preventing the tube from being pushed back in. Somehow he had to make the hole in my neck wide enough for the tube to be replaced. I asked if the tube could stay out, which was a vain hope that I might be rid of the wretched thing. It would be too risky not to have a safeguard airway of a tracheostomy tube and so it had to be returned to its former position.

    I explained that the ideal tube was that of the other manufacturer. After a rummage in the store cupboard, a nurse returned with the alternative more suitable tube. Why had it not been changed before? I had been going on for ages about having the wrong type of tube, now out of my neck, as being a problem. I might just as well have not bothered and I had been right to doubt the senior nurse's lack of dynamism. Rarely will I criticise my care because in general it was excellent. But this really pissed me off. Words like stupid git, wally…..the language gets worse….went through my head. Getting irritated couldn't save me from the current situation and at least on the plus side was the fact that I had a good trusting relationship with the surgeon.

    I had to lie flat on my bed with one pillow behind my head. My dad was on one side of the bed, the surgeon, his junior and a nurse on the other. I didn't know what was coming next, which was probably just as well. Dilators were the order of the day. These are hollow plastic tubes, narrow and pointed at one end. The idea of dilators is to shove them through the neck to increase the size of the hole leading to the windpipe. You start off with the smallest tube and progressively increase the tube size until the hole is big enough. The first went through my neck. The pain was excruciating. Not just in my neck but going all the way along the lines of my jaw to my ears. This dilator tube stayed in place for about a minute before removal. Then it was on to the next size up. When the tubes were left in my neck, I could see them pulsating in time with my neck arteries and heart beat. I can remember squeezing my dad's hand tight with each tube insertion and another memory is of me being particularly aware of the Antiques Roadshow playing on a neighbouring television. I must have been trying to distract myself from what was happening. The surgeon asked if I was okay and then he jokingly remarked how I could do backstroke swimming with a dilator in my neck as a snorkel. It was all in good humour and in many ways a way to get through this. Any distraction was welcome. He knew me well and he appreciated that I could probably get through this horror without having to go to the operating theatre. The London surgeon who did the main airway reconstruction operation with him would have undoubtedly told him of the episode of slipped cartilage. This situation here was not a life or death one, though. It was nonetheless a stressful situation. It had been better to tolerate the pain and not panic rather than go to theatre for a general anaesthetic. Much as I liked the buzz of the general anaesthetic injection, I was not that much of a "g.a." junkie.

   The tracheostomy tube was finally replaced successfully on the ward after several dilator rammings. It's a good job that the surgeon and I got on well. I think that there was a mutual admiration between us, as well as a mutual thinking of how life can deal bad hands sometimes and here we go again proving the point. I didn't feel any annoyance towards him. He had saved me from another unplanned general anaesthetic and had fixed the problem. I should rather thank him for yet again sorting out a problem with my tracheostomy tube. I felt more for him being dragged into hospital on a Sunday afternoon. It was yet another adventure on my hospital journey. At least I had the correct type of tube in place, at long last.

   I saw the registrar of the consultant surgeon a few days later in passing. He commented on how well it had been handled and was even complimentary of my tolerance to the thrusting of dilators through my neck. I could tell from his expression that it had been quite a graphic and almost gruesome experience. I think that he was surprised that we managed to pull things off without needing a general anaesthetic or at least sedation. Let's not forget my dad in all this. It must have been pretty damn awful for him to see his son having such a thing done to him. What a man. What a team. We had got through a lot together. The spirit was strong. It had not been defeated, despite a great deal of trying.

Chapter 26

Did the holiday insurance pay up? What was the excuse now?

Fortunately, I had taken out some travel insurance before my skiing holiday. One would expect that I would get near the maximum payment for the injuries incurred. At least I had not died, although then I would probably have got the maximum amount unless there was something in the small print. Not much use to me then, but it would have even so paid for a good funeral. Bit morbid, aren't I? The insurance did pay for the hospital expenses in France and the air ambulance home. What was of interest now was how much money I would get for my injuries. This was separate to the legal case in France where we were claiming from the ski-resort for alleged negligence. The maximum monetary award from the insurance was £15 000. The solicitors in Bristol who were working on the French legal case were also dealing with the insurance company.

It was taking a fair amount of negotiation. These insurance companies obviously don't cough up the cash very freely. They were trying to get away with awarding me a very small amount or even nothing at all. In order to qualify for a large payment, you had to be unable to work. At the time of the negotiations, I was in the middle of rehabilitation at Odstock Hospital and still had my throat problem, having not had the major throat operation to correct things. The insurance company's argument was that if you could move your head, you could still work because you could hold a pen in your mouth to write. This made my inability to speak less significant. It is almost laughable how outrageous and insulting these arguments were. Apparently, our solicitor gave some choice words over the telephone and the insurance company then agreed to pay out £12 500. It was good at least to get some money. £12 500 is not a large amount when you have a whole life ahead in a wheelchair with all its added expense. To put it into context, the cost of a new posh lightweight wheelchair is about £1 500 and it only lasts a few years if regularly used. But nonetheless the payment was something good to happen. It was certainly better than nothing. What a struggle it had been, though, to get some compensation when in a vulnerable enough situation already. Still, yet another experience along the way.

Chapter 27

How did the retrial in France go?

As this chapter begins with "I hate lawyers," it should give a clue to how the retrial went. There is more to it than just losing, though. Here goes with a further tragic tale. We had this top-notch French lawyer preparing the case. My dad was notified of the result by the Bristol solicitor firm and he had to tell me it. The lawyer in France had been due to present the case just after lunch on the designated trial day and for some reason he didn't even turn up. In all intents and purposes, the retrial did but did not happen. The upshot was that no compensation was coming my way. What a bummer, to say the least. I berated lawyers and French people even more than usual; and my dad joined in with vigour for the latest bit of bad luck that life had inflicted.

There were two options now available. One was to forget about any further legal proceedings. The other was to sue the French lawyer for not presenting the case and then somehow get the initial case heard again. It was all getting terribly complicated and, more importantly, expensive. I was in the middle of hospital rehabilitation and this legal wrangling was an added unwanted stress. My dad and I discussed what we thought might be the best way forward. We decided to drop legal proceedings and to concentrate on getting on with the rebuilding of my life. I think that this was a wise choice in retrospect. There was plenty to be angry about already, but a further failed legal case and extra expense might make us bitter. Fortunately, we had not reached that place called bitterness yet.

The solicitors did reimburse the money we paid for the French lawyer to prepare the retrial, but it was scant consolation. I felt even more cheated than before, but I had to put this into the past. I had to focus on the important things ahead. Money would have helped; but what can you do when it appears that things are destined to be against you? I was far more content to have been lucky with my brain injury recovery and the like than with the legal case. These situations put things into perspective and show what is truly important in life. There are indeed more precious things in life than money. It was easier to move on in my life without compensation and having no brain damage rather than the other way around. Lasting bitterness and anger had been prevented by our decision to abandon legal proceedings at an appropriate stage. The fact that I actually don't hate lawyers after all and simply consider the events part of my learning experience is good evidence of that.

Chapter 28

What was my future? Medicine wanted and a tale of two cities

It was early on in the year 1993. I had reached the stage in hospital where I could be fairly mobile and do most self-care. I would only discover whether I could be fully independent out of hospital when I had a home to go to and put all my learned skills from hospital to the test. When I had a home to go to; doesn't that sound desperate? But things were pretty desperate. I had to find a place back in society. I needed a suitable home to house me when I had significant physical impairments. I was dramatically altered physically. I was no longer this happy-go-lucky 21 year old man who didn't have these physical barriers with which to contend. How much I could do in a day would only be discovered by trying to live independently when out of the hospital. At least I could now speak, which made interacting with people far easier than before and it meant that a return to medical school was a realistic possibility if I wanted to do this. So much to consider at a young age. Surely life could be easier than this. On the same note, though, I guess that some people get it tougher than me. "There's always someone worse off than you, remember that," I hear the wise old man tell me.

     I had to assume that I would be able to do a full day's work, even though I was far from the optimal level of stamina for that at this stage. I had to have a positive attitude that things would be okay. I had already done lots of thinking about my past, present and future in my hospital stay so far. This had not necessarily been about getting an education or a job. I would often question myself about whether I could survive out of the hospital and be integrated back into society. I had been preoccupied with my physical injuries and operations, and learning wheelchair and other basic skills. These things had been so difficult, even in the hospital. The prospect of full integration away from hospital had almost seemed hopeless when I couldn't speak. Now that I had had the throat operation, I needed to think about my future in a much wider perspective than just basic rehabilitation.

Admittedly, the throat operation was not guaranteed to be a permanent success but as already mentioned I had to be positive and look forward to other things in my life.

    I had to approach what I wanted to do for a job from various angles. Firstly, it had to be enjoyable and something that I wanted to do rather than simply for the necessity of earning a living. Secondly, it had to be something that I could do. I needed to work in a wheelchair accessible environment. Also, I had to feel that the job was worthwhile. It had to be something that I could do well rather than just doing it. Thinking about whether people would be willing to employ a person in a wheelchair rather than a person not affected in my way was a consideration. I felt that I would have a harder time getting a job than most. I already had a BSc degree but I sensed that people would always have some discrimination against me. I needed to be better qualified, although I was not duty bound to do medicine as a career. This was plainly clear to me after much staring out at the Wiltshire hills and up at hospital ceilings; in other words, lots of time just to think. I had enjoyed the medical training that I had done so far and I did very much like meeting different people. Fuelling my desire to try medicine as a career was that there are so many fields of medicine from which to choose. Surely there would be some suitable for me. Also, through my experiences I might have some insight to use in working as a doctor. I could be in a unique position to practise medicine well and to affect attitudes of staff and patients. Hospitals are in the main accessible and all these reasons are why it made sense to try to return to medical school. Having a medical degree would be useful all the same, even if I didn't end up practising as a doctor.

    Where was I going to go? Bristol or London? I thought that Bristol was the more sensible choice. My family was in Bristol, Bristol was a more accessible city and my as yet unfinished adapted cottage was just outside Bristol. On the other hand, though, staff and friends at my London medical school had been very supportive and encouraging. It was not an easy decision between the two cities but on balance it was better to have close family nearby to help and to try to get a place on the Bristol course. My dad kindly organised a meeting for me to have with the Undergraduate Dean of Bristol University Medical School early in 1993. I met him and told him my reasons for wanting to return to medical school and why I wanted to change to Bristol. I also let him know where I was with my throat operations, hospital rehabilitation and planned discharge from hospital later in the year.

He told me about the Bristol University Medical School curriculum and what the facilities were like. I would be able to transfer because I already had a degree, although he needed to discuss my case with the other decision-makers in the medical school first. If they agreed, I could start there in September. I would have to do three years, which meant repeating almost a year already done. Time didn't really bother me, though. In fact, it would be useful to repeat a year because the extra year would give me the opportunity to get used to a full day and to learn how to examine patients from my wheelchair. The three years remaining would be based mainly in hospitals rather than in lecture theatres. The plan was for me to have attachments in Bristol hospitals instead of further afield because of the need to be close to my home base. Adaptations would also be made to improve access to the medical school library and to the social area of the main hospital in central Bristol. The start date of September was provisional, which allowed for any problems that I might run into before then. Still, it was exciting to have a distant date for getting on with things other than purely rehabilitation.

Chapter 29

First proper assessment since the major throat operation

The morning of the first throat assessment had come. It was early February 1993. The surgeon from London was again coming down to Salisbury to do the assessment. This date had been a focus in my mental diary for quite some time. It could at last be the day that I got rid of my troublesome tracheostomy tube. I was on a manually propelled shower chair in the shower that morning contemplating this possibility. I heard a knock at the shower door. This was unusual. The knock sounded again. I could also hear a muffled voice through the noise of running shower water. It seemed important enough for me to stop the shower, cover myself with a towel and wheel over to unlock the door.

It was one of the nurses and it wasn't good news. Even so, she was very good at breaking it because she actually did sound genuinely upset for me. Most of the staff on the ward knew the significance of the operation for me. She started off by saying how she knew of the operation's importance and how sorry she was, but the surgeon from London had had a car accident on the evening just gone. When driving home late after a lecture, he had been injured in a car crash and sustained a fractured sternum, that's breast bone to the medically-uninitiated. This meant that the operation was not going to happen today. I was really disappointed but fortunately remembered not to shoot the messenger. The operation was to be delayed until the next month. I can remember thinking to myself that someone somewhere was really trying to test my resilience.

A month went past and the operation date again arrived, now early March 1993. I was not taking anything for granted realising that anything could happen. Just please let the operation take place, I kept thinking to myself. This time there was no knock on the shower door, although purely out of superstition I tried not to stay in there long. What a relief it was to be greeted by the London surgeon when eventually in the anaesthetic room. We exchanged pleasantries and it was rather ironic for me to ask after his recovery from his accident. Life is strange sometimes, I suppose. But I was in his hands today despite me asking after his health. The Salisbury throat surgeon, present at the first operation, was also there. They were a brilliant team and I felt that I got on with them both very well.

It was quickly explained that they would have a look at the operated part of my windpipe while I was under general anaesthetic and hopefully things would look good. They would need to remove the plastic stent put in the windpipe at the original operation. Then they would probably need to laser at any narrowed areas of windpipe or scar tissue that didn't look mature enough. Only if things looked really good would they be able to remove my tracheostomy tube. Even so, it was a possibility.

The next bit was my general anaesthetic fix. The clock-face blurred and my head became progressively muzzier as I drifted off to sleep from the anaesthetist's syringe of drugs. The next thing that I knew I was in the recovery room going through my rapid sequence soberisation. When I had recovered sufficiently from the anaesthetic, the surgeons told me what had happened. Yet another peculiarity on my part was the stent going missing. I must have coughed it up without noticing since the previous operation. Goodness knows how I did this, but I must have done so. The windpipe was about eight-tenths its usual aperture. Most of the operation site looked good, although there were some angry-looking areas. The relevant sites of granulation tissue were lasered and the tracheostomy tube had to remain in place because of this. It would be another three months' minimum with a tracheostomy tube and all its hassles, but at least things were heading in the right direction.

I had to put things into perspective. The operation's outcome could have been a lot worse. There was a good likelihood that the tube could be removed at the next procedure. Also, it looked as if I might be one of the lucky four of five in who the operation is a lasting success. Again I would tell the impatient side of me to get perspective. "Don't jump the gun, Wells. Respect these experts who have restored your speech. If all goes well, this restoration will be permanent and life with a guaranteed voice and without a tube will be a reality." What a gift to have speech again. Reflecting on things years later, this ability is truly a fantastic gift. As well as the increased independence gained from being able to speak, appreciating the preciousness of this function first-hand is a great attribute to have. Not many people have that. It makes me grateful for what I have got rather than thinking about what I haven't got. Maybe that's why I don't grieve morbidly over my spinal cord injury. Certainly, my experience of not speaking has deepened me as a person significantly. I'm grateful for that. You see, positives can come out of what seem to be terrible negatives on the surface. I wouldn't wish a tracheal stricture, a.k.a. windpipe narrowing, on anyone. However, now that I have come out the other side, I am in many ways glad that I had one. I met two wonderful surgeons and the lessons learned are priceless.

The next operation was scheduled for June. In the meantime, I had to concentrate on getting ready for discharge from hospital and learning to live in the outside world as a wheelchair user. It was likely that I would still have a tracheostomy tube when I went home, but there was hope that it might be removed before I started at Bristol University Medical School in September. Better to prepare to tackle life outside the hospital than to get preoccupied by my throat, difficult as this was.

Andrew, a good friend of mine already mentioned, visited me in the afternoon. He brandished a bottle of champagne to celebrate me getting rid of the tube. We're not hooray Henrys, yuppies or whatever they're called these days. It was going to be such a significant day if I had got rid of the wretched tracheostomy tube, that a champagne celebration would have just touched the surface. He could not believe it when he saw the tube still in my neck. He seemed almost more disappointed than me. When I went through how things were going in the right direction, he seemed less down. I think that he could see then that this was a gradual journey with no wonder cures. I had had the best possible treatment for the windpipe narrowing so far and the progress with it was encouraging. Things could have been very different. Thinking of the positives here instead of the negatives certainly helped everyone involved. Andrew and Ellie visited me at home the following weekend and they bought me a fantastic stereo system with some funds that they had raised for me. Retail therapy can also help, I guess.

Chapter 30

16 March: a good or a bad day?

It was 16 March 1993. My mum, sister Lucy and niece Charlotte aged six months visited me on the ward. It had been a year since my accident. My mum said slightly nervously that she didn't know whether I would mind the fact that she had brought something with her to commemorate the occasion. Hidden in one of her bags was a small bottle of champagne, which she said was to celebrate me still being around and not dying on the many times that I came close. She was right in doing this. From now on, 16 March was almost like a new birthday for me. Even though I had had this terrible accident, it was a very real miracle that I was still around. We didn't want to make a scene and my mum tried to open the bottle under the bed covers. A loud pop sounded when the cork was pulled free. Nobody else on the ward took much notice. She then poured champagne into three plastic glasses and hid the half-full bottle somewhere inconspicuous. My mum and sister had only partially full glasses, as they hadn't decided who was going to do the driving home yet. We made a toast and it was pretty special to be doing this. I was alive, I was talking and I wasn't permanently brain-damaged: what progress from the depths.

My mum started to giggle after a few sips. Apparently, she had had very little to eat. Well, that's her excuse in any case. She was completely drunk. Lucy and I said in unison, "You're pissed, completely drunk." My mum attempted to hush us with a slurred whisper, as drunks do, and giggled some more. Then tears of laughter came to her eyes. Perhaps it was all the emotion of the occasion. Certainly we had to take the champagne away from her now. We couldn't believe how easily intoxicated she had become. The decision on who was driving home had now been made. Lucy was of course going to be the driver, although my mum did seem to sober up after a few minutes. It had been a good way to spend part of the day. I was able to enjoy time again with people important to me.

From now on, every 16 March would be a rest day for me. It is a time for me to take a day away from the rigours of life, a time for me to slow down, ponder and contemplate my life and what I have been through. Before my accident, I would occasionally go to the golf course on my own to play a few holes. It was an ideal way for me to collect my thoughts in a kind of solitude in peaceful surroundings. I need to capture this feeling again, at least on this special day. Singer Natalie Merchant communicates this escapism beautifully in the lyrics of her song, "Where I go," from the album Tigerlily when she sings about going to a secluded riverbank to unwind by letting her worries flow away in the river.

Chapter 31

June 1993: released from the hospital, still much to be achieved

The date of me leaving the hospital had arrived. Much had happened in the time since being thrust into hospital the previous year. Eight general anaesthetics had been administered and there were still some more to come. A tracheostomy tube remained, but I had the ability to speak again. My paralysis would likely be shackles for me to carry for the remainder of my life, although I had still not become adjusted to it. I might eventually adjust to it, but I would never fully accept it. I would often say to myself that I would cycle over twenty miles to work each day or be broadcast naked to millions on the television if I could have my paralysis reversed for doing so. It would be wrong for me to say that I would get over what has happened. I have just had to learn to live a different life from before. There will always be some sad reflection and bad times that I will have when thinking about how things could be different; but these memories become less painful and intense with time. Things will not change, no matter how much reflection or wishing I do.

  I did think, however, that it would only be fair for me to get some payback from my accident. I used the numbers relating to my accident and my birthday for the first ten weeks of the lottery in the hope of a jackpot win. I believe that these numbers have never even won ten pounds since the lottery's inception. They are probably the most unlucky numbers around: extremely bad superstitious value comes with them. At least I saved money by only playing the numbers for the first few weeks. Who in any case said that life was fair? It is about trying to balance the bad with the good, the rough with the smooth, and not about fairness.

  I could have stayed in hospital for longer to learn walking with calipers, but this would have delayed things a couple of months more. The thought of walking with calipers was not really important for me. Also, I wouldn't be able to walk long distances in them, no matter how good I became. It wouldn't have added much function to my life. A choice had had to be made. I had spent enough time in hospital already and I still needed to learn much about life survival from a wheelchair, which is why I decided that it was better to leave hospital and get on with my life.

When I had been released from hospital, I had to learn to regain my independence in the real world away from the artificial environment of the hospital. The building work on the cottage had not been completed, so for the first month or so I was destined to live behind the curtains in my parents' living room. I had fantastic support and I would go out on trips with trusted people and of course also with the portable tracheostomy tube suctioning machine. The return to medical college was planned for September and I had to learn how to drive and how to move my wheelchair confidently in foreign environments before then. I also needed to build up stamina to endure a day's work, something I had not done for well over a year. Before my accident seemed so distant in the past and I was a different person now. Three months did not seem like a long time before college loomed, but it was long enough to give me confidence in looking after my new self. It would be July 1993 when my cottage was ready to be moved into, and this happened to be a big progression. I would no longer feel like the lodger downstairs in my parents' living room. Things could be much better organised in my own place and furnishing a house turned out to be quite fun. It's better to have some fun and not simply to struggle.

The main event ahead other than college and independent living after leaving hospital in early June 1993 was another throat operation a couple of weeks into June. It was the second throat operation since the major one in December 1992. The operation was to evaluate whether my wretched tracheostomy tube could be removed and my hopes for this were high. Even so, I was pleased that I could speak and didn't want to take this for granted. I did not want to tempt any further fate considering what had happened to me the previous year. It soon became apparent to me that I was only able to concentrate on two or three goals for the future at one time, which were independent living, college and throat at that particular time. It was all that I could handle. In general terms, I don't think that this is a very different situation to me now as I write this book in the year 2000. There is only so much I can take on and usually there are not more than two to three principal goals. It's just that the goals and my life have shifted, which make things seem different.

Chapter 32

Later in June 1993: second throat assessment since the main operation

I had been home for a couple of weeks surviving behind the curtains in my parents' living room before I had to return to hospital for an operation. I had an overnight bed on the familiar ward in the Spinal Injuries Unit, my old home almost. Again I met the two throat surgeons in the anaesthetic room. After I told them how my speech and breathing had been going, the operation routine was quickly explained. Whether the tracheostomy tube came come out all depended on how the scarring looked on the inside of my windpipe. The next thing was to put me off to sleep (yet again), have the operation and then slowly rouse to consciousness in the recovery room. It's quite funny how you go through different stages of consciousness when rousing. First you know where you are, then you can recognise people, then you can speak but you know it will be confused words, and then you can speak sensibly. I can remember seeing a junior doctor in the recovery area who had worked at the Spinal Injuries Unit when I had been there as an in-patient. He was seeing to another patient. I wanted to call out to him but I had no words. Then when I had words, I still didn't call out, simply because I knew that I would talk drivel. When I reached the stage where I could have talked sensibly, he had gone. Frustrating or what! Never mind. What really mattered was how the operation had gone and whether my tracheostomy tube was still there.

    I had not been aware of the tube being in my neck, but I was still slightly drowsy from the anaesthetic. The London throat surgeon came to see me in the recovery room and he explained that he had had to leave the tracheostomy tube in place. The airway was wider than before, about ninety five percent of its normal aperture. There were, however, a couple of areas of quite vascular-looking granulation tissue and some associated inflammation. For this reason, he had had to keep the tracheostomy tube in place below the surgery site. The next assessment was to be in October. I mentioned about medical school beginning in September and how it might be difficult with a tracheostomy tube. He could tell my disappointment and tried to placate me by saying that things were at least heading in the right direction. We were unable to discuss things in ideal circumstances due to the location, my slight drowsiness from the anaesthetic and the surgeon having to rush back to London.

    I was at home the following weekend feeling a little downhearted. The telephone rang. It was the surgeon and he wanted to explain again why the tracheostomy tube needed to remain. He empathised with me and said that he also disliked tracheostomy tubes and wanted to remove them whenever possible. The conversation was much clearer than it had been in the recovery room. It reminded me that he was on my side, not that I ever really questioned this. He had made it possible for me to regain my speech. However, when you are grasping for every glimmer of hope, even if not immediately deliverable, it is easy to lose sight of the fact that the doctor is working with you. Empathy and showing a motivation to help as a doctor is vital and may be strengthening for the patient, especially in difficult circumstances. This was a valuable lesson for me to take on board and to remember it in my potential future career as a doctor. An article which I wrote regarding this incident was published in the British Medical Journal a few years on. My lesson will have hopefully affected other doctors' practice, as well as my own. Unfortunately, I wrongly quoted the operation in the article as the first assessment rather than the second one but this didn't make the message conveyed any different. Also, I suppose that I am allowed the odd mistake when I've had so many operations to remember. I very much valued the opportunity to write to the surgeon with the article. It was a good reason to use to let him know of my gratitude, my progress and how significant an impact his treatment had had on my life.

    It was also not all bad news from this particular operation because at least the operation had again been progress in the right direction. Despite the tracheostomy tube remaining, the probability of its removal at the next assessment was very high. College and moving into my cottage lay ahead before the next operation. The main challenges that I had already set myself to achieve before college started were driving, negotiating less than ideal wheeling surfaces and staying in my wheelchair for most of the day were. After all, I needed to be adequately independent and physically fit in order to return to college. I had somehow hoped that these things would have been less of an obstacle by having my tracheostomy tube removed because having a tube was in itself physically tiring. However, the tube hadn't been removed and now I had to adjust to the reality of having to tackle my return to college with it still in place.

Chapter 33

How did I move on after such a bad accident?

"In a wheelchair," I hear the jokers say! However, if I'm serious about it, accidents probably sound less traumatic than they actually are and it is only when you are the person involved in some way that the true horrors become apparent. Both the incidents in the early stages and the long-term consequences can only be fathomed when you are there.

My story could be summarised as a student doctor in his early-twenties breaking his back when on a skiing holiday and returning to finish his studies after recovering in a Spinal Injuries Unit. That is, however, too simplistic. It only touches the surface. It doesn't cover all the other injuries that I sustained. It does not tell of my different aims and emotions along the way. It does not tell of the inspirational people that I met: the fellow patients, family, friends, medical personnel, and medical school support and fundraising. It does not tell of all the other people who suffered and worried while I was trying to recover. The last group probably had a harder time than me. They could see how ill I was at times when I couldn't always do this. They didn't know what I was thinking or feeling all the time. They might have had to be careful about what they said as well as having to try to not appear upset or angry in front of me in case it affected me adversely when I was very weak and vulnerable. I certainly empathise with how difficult their situation must have been and am so grateful for their undying support and outward optimism.

Obviously, I myself need to be optimistic to get on and achieve my goals and certainly the attitudes of people close to you do rub off and can affect how you approach your situation. All the important ones in my case didn't express irrational rage and helped me concentrate on the future. They were non-judgemental and open-minded, which gave me the freedom to take my time to decide where my life was heading as I underwent hospital rehabilitation. And I sure did some thinking! Yes indeed. This experience is one where you can truly find yourself, think what really matters and consider the good things that you have. I was never pressurized, outside the daily rigours of the physiotherapy gym and the making of my bed on the ward (I hate making beds – who likes it, in all honesty?), with what I was to do with my life. I wasn't encouraged to dwell on the past, even though one needs some reflection and grief to soothe the psychological scars of a life-altering accident. There's a fine balance between past reflection and pathological grieving.

One needs to try to draw strength from experiences to do something positive with one's life. Life is too long to waste it doing aimless things. I personally need a purpose to occupy me. My mum said something that was truly strengthening for me one day when a bit of self-doubt had crept in about my capabilities. "Look Tom. If you decide to do something, you as much as anyone will be able to achieve it. Whenever you have really put your mind to something, you have done it well." My parents support me through thick and thin, but this went beyond that. My mum knows me better than most people and I know her pretty well, too. The honesty in what she said was very apparent and her undying faith in my capabilities and strength of character was more than just a compliment. It told me that I could do many things with my life if I really wanted and tried to do so.

Having lost my voice for a few months shortly after my accident had certainly opened my eyes, or more appropriately my ears, to what was important for me to function in life. At no time did I think that I wasn't going to regain my voice. I don't know why. Maybe I was too busy thinking about other things to worry because I had needed to get used to using a wheelchair and build up my weight and stamina when over my life-threatening injuries. Getting my voice back meant that I could have a try at returning to medical school and this challenge approached soon after I had been released from hospital. I felt fortunate to have the opportunity to tackle this challenge and there were other things for which I am deeply grateful. I was alive, I was no longer in hospital, I could speak even though I still had a tracheostomy tube in place and I had the best family that you could ask for. These situations certainly make you appreciate the things that you have got and which may not have been fully valued before. There was a lot to be thankful for.

I had come a long way and I hope in future that I don't forget how ill I was and from where I have come by becoming too ambitious at the cost of losing appreciation for the important things in life. It did not matter greatly if medical school was unsuccessful. When you have almost died on more than one occasion, I think that there isn't much that can destroy you psychologically. This is probably because every day from then on is treated as a bonus. It would be a disappointment if medical school didn't go well, but I would get over it. I think the one thing that could affect me greatly would be someone very close to me dying. All my grandparents have died but I was quite young when this happened. I was close to them but somehow things seem different when you are an adult. I dearly love my parents and siblings. Contemplating one of their deaths is something that I find scary because I don't know exactly how I will react to it. It is something unknown to me; fortunately, I guess. Thinking this, I can only imagine how hard it must have been for them when I was very ill. For all I know, they might still grieve me being in a wheelchair rather than being a healthy young man walking. You can rarely discuss things completely but we all inherently know each of us has different scars. I feel for their scars, whatever they may be, even if I don't go out of my way to tell them.

I had lots of people concerned for my wellbeing. People would pray for me, including the churchgoers in my parents' village. In addition to this, there was a nun who was based in a convent near Oxford. I had been put forward to have her praying for me regularly. I was almost chosen as a project for her. She used to communicate with my mum and vice versa at times when I was either not so well or had an operation. I am still in contact with her years after the accident and have even visited her at the convent.

There was help for me from many sources. Even though certain things cannot be changed no matter how much reflection, I believe that prayer can be helpful. I am only too aware of this being my belief, so will expect criticism in this not being established fact. But, a lot of what I've written is down to my interpretation of events, so please don't slag off the whole book. Even so, many people praying for me gave me strength at times, bonds people together, and it might have helped my parents and others, too.

People might ask in religious arguments or discussion, depending on their disposition, "If you believe in God, then why would God or whatever you believe in do this?" I am a religious person but it isn't necessary for me to divulge all details of my religious beliefs here. It's personal and so might be difficult to communicate and also it doesn't add a great deal to the story. What does matter is that when needed my religious beliefs alongside other sources of strength have empowered me to cope. I don't believe that God dishes out bad and good things willy-nilly. People have some control over their actions and bad things can happen as a result of this autonomy. The God in which I believe gives me strength to try to work through difficult times. There is one particular passage in the Bible, which reminds me of the strength that I can unknowingly receive in adversity. In the passage, somebody is questioning God about God not always being there to help him. God denies the accusation. The man then asks God where God had been when he was in his time of most need, as there was only one set of footsteps visible in the sand at that moment. God replies that it was then that God was carrying him. I feel that I have been carried on many occasions during my journey. Somebody has carried me through all my brushes with death and other testing times.

    If I had died, it would not have been God letting me down. Success is not simply life rather than death. Success is about having valuable experiences from which to learn. If I had died, it would have been dreadful for my family but they would still have their memories of me. My death might have made the family even closer, it might have inspired them to do something amazing that they would otherwise not have done or it might have tested their beliefs to a positive effect. There are many things that might have come out of my demise. Things are not all plainly black and white, good and bad. It seems strange to be talking about my death when I'm alive. I don't think that things always happen for a reason, although some things can nevertheless have many different effects, some of which are unexpected. Then, when reflecting on an event, it might be considered by people as having had a reason. If this helps people, I don't mind it being reason or effect. I hope that all this isn't too contradictory or confusing. I confuse myself sometimes. Language can tie me in knots. It's only my analysis, so feel free to disagree. I had better not talk too much about religion and suchlike, as people can be unenthused by evangelical talk. Worth mentioning it, though, because it's an important part of me and my recovery from illness.

I have never really cried or done whatever is expected when such a terrible life-altering event has occurred to an individual. That doesn't mean that I wasn't upset by what had happened to me on that fateful skiing holiday. My adjustment seemed to be a controlled grief; but was it too controlled? I am only too aware that different people handle things differently. There shouldn't be a prescribed way to deal with grief, although there are sometimes judgements as to whether it happens the right or wrong way. It is difficult to make generalisations in these situations. There is also no need for me to explain normal and abnormal grief reactions to communicate why I worried about how I reacted. It did indeed worry me that because I had not broken down in a screaming or crying frenzy that there might be future consequences.

As can be seen, there are many things that I have had to deal with in my new life. I had to deal with a whole new life. I have not cursorily put behind me what has happened. My situation has been a dreadful thing to which to have to adjust. I have tried to move on and I think that I have done pretty well. Despite this, I still wondered whether it was unhealthy to grieve without floods of tears. I kept expecting to have a breakdown because I had not poured out grief and anger. "Why me? Life is unfair. If only. My life has been ripped in pieces." These thoughts entered my head but there was no real hatred, blame or hysteria at any stage.

These accidents tend to be indiscriminate. After all, if you knew something bad was going to happen, you would avoid it. Then no accident would happen. What am I trying to say? No one deserves to be injured in the way that I was. After much contemplation since my accident, I have realised that life is often unfair. There's no use trying to change what life does, but there is much to be said for trying to make the most of the circumstances in which you find yourself. In many ways, it's almost like fighting against life's apparent injustice. It must be said, though, that alongside life's unfairness there is a great deal of beauty, too. I now believe that enduring all this suffering has resulted in a greater good coming out of my life and, after almost dying, I'm just glad to be here and every day is a gift for me to treasure. I'm paralysed but have a good quality of life, probably most to do with my changed attitude to life. There is so much to enjoy about life and this can be especially appreciated when you know how bad life can get. Also, almost dying has somehow given me a confidence to live life with even more optimism than before. There is no longer the hidden worry about dying. Life is indeed for enjoyment and furthering my self-discovery. Life challenges have become welcome. It is now so much clearer to me that the reason for the range of emotions is for this self-discovery process to occur. Grief has as much a purpose as joy in this.

From soon after leaving hospital, I wrote things down about my innermost thoughts and feelings. This certainly helped in my catharsis and in informing me of how I felt about myself. It also helps remind me now of how fraught some of the experiences were, when time can make memories become less accurate vague recollections. All this writing down made me more aware of how I felt about all that had happened. Since my catharsis had been achieved already by doing this, the purpose of writing a book was primarily for letting those close to me know how I have appreciated all that was done for me. I wrote it before getting a publisher, so that my writing style wouldn't be swayed by a publisher's pressure. Let's hope that I manage to communicate the rawness of what has happened to me and at the same time capture the idea that all is not lost in adversity.

Much can be achieved with the necessary opportunity, belief and optimism to have a productive life. Early on, having lots of time in hospital away from the outside pressures of the world for my recovery, when I could just contemplate things, was beneficial. It helped me get what had happened to me into my head in my own time. I was only able to look properly at my life ahead when I had sorted out how I felt about me in my new situation. The time in hospital was in a strange way almost like a retreat, kind of like the sort in which religious figures partake occasionally. It was in many ways, other than the obvious outward insults on my physical state, a very special period of my life.

Who knows what's the best way to move on? Admittedly, I have semi-jokingly slagged off some people along the way: the French, the lawyers, the doctors in France who inserted my tracheostomy tube, the ski-resort, the French again, the vandals who destroyed the hut protection and then some people who I have encountered on my story so far. This book is not a place for me to point the finger and pass blame on individuals, especially since I believe that no one has been actively vindictive. It's better to learn from experiences, rather than getting obsessed with blaming someone or something. The best thing for me to do is to grow through my pain. The hurt hasn't felt good but hopefully my character the other side has been enriched and made stronger through it all. I think that it has, but really only other people can tell me that.

      The blame game doesn't benefit anyone and at the centre of my handling things is humour. My parents and others close to me have never been outwardly bitter. Bitter is a horrible word and it describes a horrible emotion to have. Humour through the bad times has been very helpful to remain positive. It's best to learn from the past, look forward to the future and then the present should be as good as it can be. Bad luck and mistakes happen to everyone in varying degrees. The phrase "if only….." can be very hindering in its philosophy. We all need a bit of a self-pitying session at times, but there is a fine line between despair and positive reflection. Think of the good things that have come from the bad. Anger tends to have a passion within it and you can only have a certain amount of energy for passions. If you are too busy being bitter, passing blame and directing anger at different people, you won't have enough energy to put it towards good and purposeful activities.

      I have found that it is far easier to move on from some crisis if the funny side can be seen. That is not to say that there is always a funny side. You can't really step aside from the issues and hope to make progress. Sometimes you need to confront important issues head-on and think through difficult decisions seriously. It does indeed help, though, not to dwell on things morbidly. Even though humour through bad times can be a good thing, I would hope that I don't walk around (ha! ha!) like a madman laughing all the time. Admittedly, I do so occasionally. Nonetheless, it's important for people to realise that even though jolly I do take seriously making the most out of my life and my opportunities. There is a balance that needs to be found. I have found it more tolerable getting through what has been a really awful experience with the aid of my own humour and that of others around. I am sure that laughing has been a healthy thing for me to do. Long may chuckles continue.

Trial and error is the way to see what you can achieve. I would set a couple of goals, try to achieve them and see where I ended up. The outcome of each goal depended mainly on my perseverance and ability rather than me having to rely on someone else for it to be achieved. This would give me a sense of control over my future. The ability to set goals required motivation but motivation didn't come easily or cheaply. Support and opportunity was needed for motivation to develop. Wishes for the future and physical capabilities change with time and they vary depending on the person. This is what makes coping with life's challenges ever-changing and personalised. I don't think that I have made any major mistakes in my choices so far since my accident and I have also been fortunate with my selection of available choices. I'm happy where I am now.

Who can tell if I would have been happier taking a different route? There should be less reflection here, though. Let me approach my life as Robin Williams encourages his students in Dead Poet's Society when he tells them to make their lives extraordinary by seizing the day, which is succinctly communicated in the phrase carpe diem. I tell myself to make the most of these words by valuing and enjoying each day and encouraging myself to do much with my life as well as encouraging others. And then it should be a good thing when I reflect on my life. Life itself should be something positively enjoyed. Encouragement and humour are far more pleasant words than bitterness and anger. You see, it's all in the attitude: encouragement, no bitterness, plenty of laughter. I feel compelled and responsible to make the most of my new life and to use what I have learned from my experiences in the best possible way.

My choices have never felt difficult for me to make and I suppose that I have not really considered myself as particularly brave. The choices have somehow seemed obvious, but I shouldn't shy away from the fact that it does take a strength of character to move on positively from the depths of paralysis. It is when people approach me to remark their amazement at my cheer and optimism, which makes me consider the way in which I have handled my situation. It isn't hard to be positive, having discovered that it is that sort of attitude which seems to work well in moving on with life. It's all the better, though, if it inspires people, too. The apparent ease at moving on is why I have been surprised when people are incredulous of my way of living. When I see people not take life head-on and slip into obscurity, it makes me realise that I have taken a challenging route in life. I don't think that I would call it courage, although I suppose that courage is rarely felt by the person displaying it. It is simply noticed by others. A good philosophy to reaffirm the worth of tackling life's challenges is that it's better to fail sometimes than to regret never trying.

      Life is indeed enjoyable, just so long as you are making a go at living it. It would be wrong if I didn't acknowledge that you do need a certain determination when there are additional challenges such as in spinal cord injury. I would be denying my own situation if I didn't admit that. After all, in the long term I have to deal with reduced mobility, inability to feel from the lower chest down, altered bladder, bowel and sexual function as well as potential fertility difficulties. It is undoubtedly tough living with paralysis but it's better to concentrate on what you can do rather than what you can't. I simply hope to continue to have determination to take a route in life which seems the right one, however hard it may be.

Chapter 34

Holiday with family in Cornwall

This holiday was going to be a test for me. Even though I was with my parents, one brother, my sister and niece, it was to be the first time since my accident that I would be away from hospital and home for several days. In fact it was pretty much going to be a test for not just me but for all of us. When would a holiday not be a test? Would it always be a test rather than fun? Whatever the case, there was always going to be some fun had on a holiday and I suppose that everyone has anxieties about their holiday being a success. From now on in my life, though, I would have added stresses with which to contend, be it on holiday or not. With time these added stresses would become accepted as routine rather than an imposition. The more holidays that I had without disaster, the less nervous I would be about how holidays would turn out.

So, off we set in two cars for our Cornish holiday destination. My luggage requirements seemed so much more significant than on previous holidays. This time I had to bring the essential portable suctioning machine and catheters for my tracheostomy tube secretions, equipment to help with my bowel and bladder management as well as wheelchair equipment. I depended on a great deal of help, both human and medical. My dad had expertly planned the trip and we were going to be staying in a holiday house on our own. It was a long journey down and I was excited to be escaping the confines of Bristol to see another place.

The holiday did indeed turn out to be more fun than worrying. Good food was enjoyed, a lot being self-catering. We visited a fair few attractions. There was a seal sanctuary where we took an open-air train ride to the top part of the complex. Then there was a monkey sanctuary and that was fantastic. Here monkeys roamed among the paying public. It was pretty exciting to wonder where the monkeys might be and very memorable. There was also a train museum, well worth a wheel around. We went on a steam train journey one day, too. We were banished to the guard's van. The windows of the carriage were barred, so we did feel slightly imprisoned, almost like caged animals. It was more an experience than a joy. My brother was lucky enough to avoid this journey. I can't remember why he did miss it and it certainly made me wonder whether he knew something that we didn't. There was my mum, dad, sister and niece in her pram crammed in this small space and we mostly saw the steamy windows of the humid carriage for the trip. When the train arrived at its destination, I summoned up enough courage to dare negotiate the slightly precarious ramps from the carriage to get on to the station platform for about half an hour. Not much to see but far better than risking going stir crazy from thirty minutes more in the guard's van, a makeshift incubator.

 Then there were a few quaint Cornish towns that we visited. Land's End was another outing on the holiday: quite commercialised but definitely worth a visit. The house in which we were staying was generally good. There was a downstairs bedroom accessible by wheelchair, although I couldn't get to the toilet properly. This necessitated me to do the undignified antics of evacuating my bowels on the bed by using suppositories and a well-placed inco pad. My brother Ali used to and still does say jokingly, "Can't you just write a complaint letter about what you thought was substandard rather than resorting to your disgusting protests?" Better to see the funny side, I suppose.

 We set off for home after a great break away. It had been a test but it had also been a really enjoyable few days. A sense of achievement as well as having had fun was felt. I left with my dad in one car, the others in the second car. After about an hour on the road, my dad realised that the suction machine had been left behind at the house. We turned back, while the others carried on home. I was very reliant on that machine, so our return to the holiday house was completed with some urgency. Luckily, my tube didn't become frothy in the meantime. It was just a nuisance to add two hours to a long journey. Happily, we were not held up on the roads behind any cauliflower heads, Doris Sunday afternoon drivers or whatever you like to call them. I think that I even did some of the driving on this occasion. All in all, we had had a good time away. It was something to give me added confidence in my capabilities, but I was still having to cope with a lot. It was bad enough learning to live with the condition of paraplegia, but my tracheostomy tube was a significant added burden. Life would be dramatically improved by being without it.

Chapter 35

September 1993: return to medical school

The next throat assessment was planned for October 2003, a month into the medical school year. This meant that I had to tolerate the tracheostomy tube and at the same time test the water for doing a day's work at medical college. This involved very early starts to mornings. What a nightmare for someone who is not a morning-type person, namely me. I hate mornings. I can remember how I would get up at the last minute when I was a student in London. It would be a quick putting on of clothes, brushing of my teeth, wetting my hair under a tap to get it in the correct position and then off to college. I would even shave the night before, so that I could get up later. I would get up at about eight-twenty for a nine o' clock start.

Mornings were very different now. There was so much more to do and I was also slightly slower than my previous sprightly self. I had the tracheostomy tube with which to contend and there was loads of gunk to suction from it early in the morning. This involved injecting saline down it to loosen the secretions while I lay flat in bed. Suctioning would then ensue. The suction session would take from around about thirty minutes to an hour. My mum used to help with this, passing me suction catheters and saline in syringes. Dressing and getting out of bed took a great deal longer than before. Typically, I would wake at before six for a nine o' clock start. My life had considerably changed from what it had been before.

The first few weeks involved a lecture block. I had my own parking space at the Bristol Royal Infirmary, which was where the lectures were being held, and my position appeared to be very privileged. It seemed almost more than some hospital consultants, not that I was trying to compete with or impress anyone. I suppose that it was only right for someone with my limited mobility to have convenient parking facilities. I had been given a key to the front entrance of the lecture theatre, since the conventional route involved going up stairs at the back of it. This meant that I couldn't arrive late inconspicuously. Was I to be teacher's pet at the front of class? Well,

I certainly had no choice other than being at the front. Let's leave it at that.

At the mid-morning coffee break on the first day, several people came up to me to chat and welcome me. Everyone was very friendly. It was quite a challenging day. It could have been very scary but I managed to put it into perspective by self-reflecting on all the other traumas through which I had been. I was a little self-conscious of my tracheostomy tube, more so than my wheelchair. This might have been because I had accepted my wheelchair as a slightly more permanent feature than my tracheostomy tube. Also, it was easier to conceal the tracheostomy tube, even though my attempts at concealing it below suitable clothing were not entirely successful. This did not worry me too much. However, I didn't want to make the tube obviously visible because some people can find them unpleasant to look at, even if they're training to be doctors. Despite the tracheostomy tube still being a strain, I did manage to soon settle in. My new medical school was treating me as well as could be possible. Nonetheless, I would usually need early evenings in bed to endure both the early morning starts and lasting a whole day in my wheelchair. It was very tiring but progress was happening.

Chapter 36

Learning to do the doctor bit as a student

My first medical attachment on the wards began just after the lecture block. I was with five other students at the Bristol Royal Infirmary for six weeks. The students in this group were very pleasant and it was an ideal time to see how difficult it would be for me to examine patients from a wheelchair. I had already practised some of the examination on my dad and other kind volunteers to figure out where the difficulties might be. It didn't appear to be impossible, and so it was good to try it on other people, namely real patients. It was useful to be doing part of the course that I had already done before. This meant that there was no great pressure to be learning new things. The main thrust for me was to learn my examination technique from a wheelchair. If I couldn't examine patients properly, I would be unable to practise proficiently as a doctor at the end of the course. By the end of the attachment, I had worked out where things were tricky and ways around them. Procedures like taking blood and cannula placement into veins were relearned. Further on in my career I would have to see if I could proficiently do other procedures such as chest drain insertions and lumbar punctures and this would probably be when I was a doctor, if I got that far. Although there was quite way to go before I became a doctor, the progress made after my first attachment made the idea of becoming one seem possible.

How did patients react to me? There was no obvious surprise from the patients at seeing me on the wards. Most of the time I don't think that they even noticed me being in a wheelchair, although very occasionally I would hear patients, and it tended to be old ladies, saying to one another, "Oh dear, poor man. What a terrible thing for him to be in a wheelchair. It's far worse than what I've got. I couldn't live like that." I would feign deafness to ignore them.

There was one occasion that I found particularly amusing. An elderly gentleman had come into the hospital with a stroke. He was weak down one side of his body and was receiving physiotherapy to optimise his independence. I went to have a chat with him one morning about how things were going. He started telling me about the physiotherapy and how hard he was finding it. He had obviously not noticed my wheelchair because he went on to say, "You don't know how hard it is down there, being pushed to do more and more." I let him go on about it a bit more because I think that he was finding it quite therapeutic, after which I pointed out that I was in a wheelchair and might have an idea of what the physiotherapy involved. I didn't labour the point, but it was nevertheless interesting and humorous to see his reaction when he could envisage the reality of my background. Assumptions obviously come from both sides in the doctor-patient relationship.

    I cannot truly know what patients think of me. I'm no mind reader, after all. In general, though, I feel that my situation can have more positive than negative aspects when interacting with patients. I have had no obvious outcries of people not wanting to be treated by me because I'm in a wheelchair. I think that they see the doctor and the person before they see the wheelchair. The thing that I have found helpful is that I can sometimes draw on aspects of my experience when dealing with patients. It's important not to overdo it, though, but there are times when it can be valuable. I think that I am also more aware than I probably would have been about hearing what patients want to say. It is possible to get a vibe as to how communication is going. Even so, not being a mind reader means that I don't know for sure and I'm quite aware that often the person who says that they are good actually isn't very good.

    One thing on which I can reflect is how comfortable I feel talking with patients about certain issues when I might have previously felt awkward. When I was a medical student in my first clinical year in London, a young man with leukemia was brought into the lecture theatre with his girlfriend. There were about forty students there, myself included. The doctor who organised the session said that the gentleman had kindly agreed to answer any questions that we might have. I can remember feeling very inadequate and really worried that I didn't have anything sensible to ask the man. I found it very scary to try to think of the right thing to ask. Now, years after my accident, I wouldn't be worried that I had nothing to ask. I wouldn't feel the need to ask something just for the sake of asking. I think that I would also probably find it easier to ask a sensible question. Along with this, I would probably listen more and feel and express empathy more appropriately to someone's situation. It's often better that way. Whether this is due to experience from my accident or from work experience of dealing with patients, I don't know. I do find it fascinating, though, to realise a change in my approach to that sort of situation. Here I am blowing my own trumpet about dealing with patients. I feel that I have just improved my own skills, yet despite this I still might not handle situations ideally and not as well as some other people. It's important that I remind myself of this and that communication as both a doctor and a member of the public is a continued learning process.

Chapter 37

October 1993: throat lasering; third time lucky?

The third windpipe assessment under general anaesthetic since the main operation happened midway through my first ward attachment at Bristol University Medical School. It was another return visit to the Spinal Injuries Unit in Salisbury. I was probably going to need lasering to some areas of scar tissue. Again my main concern was getting rid of the tube, although I was only too aware that I should just hope for the windpipe to look no worse than at the previous operation. If I failed to remind myself of this, it was easy to get hungry for progress and to be disappointed. This had been learned from the experience of the previous two operations. I suppose wisdom does indeed come through experience.

    I met the two throat surgeons in the anaesthetic room yet again, just before my general anaesthetic injection. They asked if I had managed to block off the end of the tube with a bung and only breathe through my mouth for long periods. I said that I had until a month ago. They looked concerned, thinking that things might have got worse in the last month. Not to keep them in suspense for long, I went on to say that I hadn't bunged off for the last month because I had lost the bung. They smiled in amused relief, although comedy is probably not my forte. The general anaesthetic world was experienced again. When I awoke this time, the tube had to my delight gone. It had been a long nineteen months that I had endured the hassle of a tube. It was a such a great feeling not to have a tube in my neck. The tube had been something that I had been paranoidly conscious about. Indeed, I probably had good reasons to have been paranoid about it. It was such a relief to be rid of it. Better not to get too excited, though, as the permanent success from all these operations was not guaranteed. The windpipe could still become narrow again. I needed to return in March 1994 for another assessment and possible lasering while under general anaesthetic, yet another fix for the hospital junky. Despite this, the windpipe scar tissue did look good on this occasion and the likelihood of cure was good. The overwhelming feeling was one of triumph. At long last the tube had gone and now my neck was naked, other than the remaining scar from my previous battles.

What a transformation to my day! It was truly marvellous. The starts to the day were about an hour later. I didn't have to mess around with saline down my windpipe and suction machines. Mess is probably an appropriate word, what with all the yock that would be suctioned from the tube. Yuck to yock! I also didn't have to change tracheostomy neck dressings. I didn't have to carry a portable suction machine in the boot of my car. I didn't have to worry about secretions blocking up my tube and airway resulting in embarrassing situations. There was less chest pain. I could think about taking up swimming. Truly marvellous does not even touch on how brilliant it was to be free of a tracheostomy tube. Admittedly, it was not quite as significant as the time that I got my speech back, but it was nonetheless a major hurdle negotiated. My life had been transformed in many ways.

Chapter 38

When would the operations stop?

My last general anaesthetic was in March 1994. When I look back at how many operations that I had in the couple of years following my accident, it makes me think, "Wow, I really have been through a traumatic experience." But I am through to the other side of it all. The fatalistic pessimist in me whispers, "For now." Let's tell the pessimist to sod off, though. I have recovered to some semblance of my former self after having been thrown down into the depths where I hardly recognised myself. Shawn Colvin manages to convey to me in the first few lines of her song "One Small Year," exactly what an unexpected strain the year of 1992/3 was. 1992/3 might have been just a year but this one small year had been a supreme fight and it had definitely taken all of me just to stay alive, let alone gaining some meaningful independence. I had been tested to the extreme. I had literally fought to stay alive having been subjected to the ultimate marathon where my life had indeed been on the line.

    I can still remember fighting for breath as my windpipe narrowed to near asphyxia when I developed my tracheal stricture. Also, I had had many operations in this time. I wrote a list soon after getting out of hospital, lest I forget them. I think if you say a number, it has less of an impact than each one listed individually. So here's the chronological league table for maximum impact:
(1) March 1992: jaws wired and tracheostomy tube inserted; (2) March 1992: back rods inserted, jaws unwired and plated, tracheostomy tube removed; (3) April 1992: reinsertion of tracheostomy tube below tracheal stricture that developed after initial tracheostomy tube removal; (4) inspection and dilatation of tracheal stricture; (5) telescope examination of bladder to look for stones under spinal anaesthetic because I appeared to be getting frequent urine infections; (6) operation to change tracheostomy tube because stricture scarring had grown into the fenestration of the tube; (7) cartilage slipping into the windpipe, when tracheostomy tube was out, necessitating an emergency operation under adequate light to replace

the tube; (8) 6 December 1992: trachea reconstruction operation; (9) March 1993: first lasering to trachea operation site; (10) June 1993: second lasering to trachea operation site; (11) October 1993: third lasering to trachea operation site and tracheostomy tube removal; (12) March 1994: fourth lasering to trachea operation site.

What a horribly long list, although bloody might be a more appropriate adjective in this instance. I had had twelve operations in two years, of which eleven required a general anaesthetic.

Finally, I had a further assessment of my trachea's progress in the ear, nose and throat outpatient clinic at Salisbury in November 1994. Here, local anaesthetic was sprayed to the back of my mouth and up my nose. This allowed a flexible telescope to be guided up my nose and down the back of my throat in the vicinity of my vocal cords while I was awake. It was intriguing to see my vocal cords on a television screen and watch them do different things as I swallowed, coughed and breathed.

Let's not also forget the occasion that my tracheostomy tube was pulled out by accident on the ward and then the other time that dilators were rammed through my neck on the ward. What a true nightmare it had been. The grass can actually sometimes be greener, though, when you get to the other side. It's true to say that it's terrifically hard to get there when life has suddenly shoved you into a desperate situation from which to recover. It literally does take all of you to get there. It's worth it, though, in order to taste some of the sweetness of the green pasture once again. Probably too many metaphors; I had better be careful not to lose my meaning within complicated language. The bottom line is that I couldn't have given any more effort when trying to survive. Fortunately I did survive.

Chapter 39

Physical pain is an issue

Despite the chest pain improving a bit after my tracheostomy tube was removed, it was still quite troublesome and physically wearing. It was mainly related to nerve damage at the level of my back fracture and also to rib fractures. This nerve type pain is known as neuropathic pain. I had tolerated it for some time, thinking that it might improve after the tracheostomy tube was removed. Pain is very much beyond the physical. It is truly grinding and mentally tiring if it is present for a long time.

    I had an appointment with a very pleasant doctor, an anaesthetist, at the pain clinic in the Bristol Royal Infirmary. What seemed a break of habit was me not coming for yet another general anaesthetic fix when I saw the anaesthetist. Instead, I had various tests looking into my problem and, after this, he went through treatment options that could be tried. There were two things with which to start. One was a pill called amitriptyline, the other was a device called a TENS machine. Amitriptyline has a couple of different uses. One is in the treatment of depression. I certainly had plenty about which to be annoyed and to get low. However, believe it or not, I wasn't depressed, although they do say that the depressed person doesn't have insight into his or her condition sometimes. The other use of amitriptyline is in the treatment of this neuropathic pain that I mentioned. It is taken in lower doses than those used in depression. An aspect of amitriptyline is sedation and this can be useful by taking it at night, if you are having difficulty sleeping; very tiresome, though, if you happen to take it to extremes and sleep all day, too. The amitriptyline took a while to take full effect. By that, I mean a couple of weeks of regular use and after regular use it did indeed help with the ever-wearing discomfort that I had been experiencing each day. When you have had to endure unpleasant pain sensations for a long time, you really appreciate it when it improves. The pain didn't disappear completely, but it was far more bearable. I would get home less tired, having had to put up less of a fight against the pain enemy.

The amitriptyline also affected my bladder and bowels, one good and one bad. For one reason or another, my bladder hadn't fitted into either of the two standard bladder management techniques adopted at a Spinal Injuries Unit. One is to wee into a urine leg-bag with a urosheath or condom over the relevant bit, if you get my drift. The other is to pop a tube up the centre of your willy into your bladder whenever you needed to empty it, known as intermittent self-catheterisation. The amitriptyline made my bladder fit more into the latter. In the beginning I was quite perturbed on hearing what intermittent self-catheterisation involved, but after getting over my initial reservations I found this method more acceptable. That's because it's almost back to previous normality of emptying my bladder. Even so, it is still far from the convenience that I used to enjoy and take for granted. Before all this crap, I had proper control and sensations for as-and-when to wee. This is no longer the same.

Now I mention the word crap, here's how the amitriptyline would affect my bowels. It would make me constipated. Laxatives were needed occasionally and maybe even a longer time was spent on the toilet. What was the difference between forty and sixty minutes, though? You can still read a book chapter in both. Life is ever complicated with all these problematic secrets. You wouldn't want to sit next to me on a train, lest I share them with you. Little chance of that. I would probably be put in the guard's van and in any case I don't make a habit of talking about bowels and bladder in public. I just write about it!!

And how did it go with the TENS machine that I mentioned? But firstly what on earth is a TENS machine? A TENS machine might be familiar to pregnant women and people with back pain. TENS stands for Transcutaneous Electrical Nerve Stimulation. That's on earth, of course. Probably on the moon, it means Totally Excellent NASA Spaceship! Now, I'm really being stupid. "Pull yourself together, Wells." The TENS machine consists of leads from a control box going to two flat rubbery pads or electrodes. You attach the electrodes to the skin with electrical conduction gel and tape on the right bits. It's quite a fiddle. You normally put them near to where the pain is and send electrical pulses of varying intensity and waveform to the electrodes. You mess around with the equipment until you find whether you get any relief. After a lot of perseverance I discovered that it did give me really good relief. It was amazing how I could turn on the machine and the annoying burning hypersensitive area on my chest would go numb. It was fantastic. Years on, I occasionally take an amitriptyline tablet and no longer need to use the TENS machine. My life has certainly improved. My pain was a hidden burden. It still is but it has less of an impact on my life now. It was another reminder for me to appreciate that many things can lie beneath a person's obvious outward appearance, behind people's curtains.

When the pain became more bearable, I could realise what a strain it had indeed been for me. My eyes were opened to yet another experience, the plight of living with chronic pain, a bad enemy. But it need not be a hopeless plight if you can get the right help. I will now certainly think hard before dismissing someone's symptoms as insignificant. If the person says that they are significant, they usually are. To empathise truly, you need to try to understand where the person in difficulty is coming from. Fortunately, that doesn't mean you always need to have experienced what they are experiencing. But, if you can draw on some aspects of your experiences for some good, you might as well.

Chapter 40

Comic moments: condoms, toilet issues and strange people

As well as being fantastically supportive, my parents and close family make me laugh a lot. There was one time in particular that springs to mind. My mother often collects prescription items for me, which include things such as urine leg-bags, catheters and urosheaths. Urosheaths, also known as condoms, are essential in preventing embarrassing accidents by attaching them to urine leg-bags when it is anticipated that lavatories will be inaccessible because you can wee into the leg-bag with everyone else none the wiser. These condom-type devices are certainly a pleasant alternative to a permanent indwelling catheter and they come in boxes of thirty. The amusing story involved my mum entering a busy chemist to collect my prescription. In a loud voice she said to the assistant, "Excuse me, have you got the two boxes of thirty condoms for my son?" I wasn't there to witness this, but according to my mum the assistant did not flinch. Even so, my mum realised her indiscretion. I think that she felt like going on to say in an even louder voice that we were very liberal and open in our family and what was wrong with her buying condoms for her son in today's free and easy society when he's a shy sex maniac. Well, she has in fact only the once made this announcement about condoms, which makes me believe that she does still have some responsibility for being socially appropriate. It had to be done just once, though, to make me still laugh when I picture her there saying, "Got two boxes of thirty condoms for my son?"

    Another time actually involved me. This again was embarrassing. I returned home in the afternoon, having finished college early. I came through my parents' front door to be greeted by my mum. "Oh, hello Tom. What are you doing?" For some reason, I answered this question with the response, "I need to have a crap." How bizarre it was. The words just came out of my mouth. She looked shocked and then loudly said that was one of her friends was there, the friend having come over to the house for afternoon coffee.

It was plenty more than bizarre now and my mouth opened aghast at what I had said. My brother was in the hall with my mum. I heard my mum's friend say "hello" from the living room. This was literally about five yards from where my rude utterances had emerged. Fortunately, a wall separated the two of us. I replied "hello" and then disappeared into the kitchen with my brother Ali. My mum returned to her guest in the living room. Having closed the kitchen door behind us, we laughed out of shock at what I had said. I could barely speak through my laughing. It was rather muffled laughter, though, as I had done enough damage already with those few words. After all, I didn't want to further my demise in the eyes of my mum's friend.

I had to go through the living room at some stage to get to my house and ultimately my bathroom. How could I go through and face my mum's friend after this? What were her and my mum talking about now? The weather? Food? Certainly not my bowels! What did my mum say when she went back in the room to her friend? Did she apologise for her son's filthy tongue? What am I like? A liability, that's for sure. Well, I did go through the living room, uttered usual pleasantries and kept a straight face before excusing myself. My poor mother; what I put her through. We have a good laugh about this now, embarrassing as it was.

These memorable incidents were happening thick and fast. The next one involved a shopping trip into central Bristol with my brother Ali. We were in John Lewis and I needed to go to the toilet. Back to toilets, yet again! I had a urinary leg-bag strapped to my inside lower leg and a condom of the drainage urosheath type was attached to the tube of the leg-bag. I simply needed to roll up my trouser leg a short distance, unlock the tap of the leg-bag and empty the bag. I was using this privilege in case I couldn't find an accessible toilet for my privacy. My brother also came into the toilet to relieve himself. I wheeled up to the urine trough and did my leg-bag emptying routine in a matter of fact manner. There was an old bloke at the trough and he observed in amazement and disbelief. His mouth dropped open as a sign of his surprise and certainly not something usually done in a gents' toilet. I met my brother outside the toilet and he couldn't believe the old man's shocked face. It was as if the man had thought that I had a rather large appendage that needed to be strapped down my leg. He probably thought that I was in a wheelchair because of problems with blood pressure or walking, owing to a willy the length of my leg. It was almost as if I should be in the Guinness book of records. His aghast face was hilarious. We pissed ourselves laughing and thank goodness for urosheaths, otherwise I might have done more than just the metaphorical.

  Another strange moment came when I was shopping again, this time on my own. When they talk of integrating disabled people in society, they don't mention these incidents. I had just come out of a record store and a black lady approached me. She was with a boy, who must have been about six years old. I think that he was her son. She asked me if I was religious. With apprehension, I indicated that I had some religious conviction. I wasn't keen on being accosted by people about faith or many other things in a busy shopping area. She went on to tell me of how she had been cured of a medical condition, after much prayer. Then, she asked me if I would mind her praying for me. Thinking that this couldn't do any harm, I agreed. I thought that she was going to go home or to her local church to do this. Naïve me! To my horror, her hand pressed on the top of my head and she started chanting various words. The young boy danced around me, waving a stick with tassels attached. Could I believe what was happening? I had nervous laughter, in particular hoping that no one I knew would see me. Even though she was only well meaning, it was really embarrassing all the same. After she had finished, I thanked her and I scurried off with head held low. Now look what a stupid mess I got myself into again. Still, it was over very quickly and there were no long-lasting effects. Sadly, it did not cure me completely as planned. C'est la vie.

  There was yet another strange incident that happened. This time I was a student on my first medical attachment at the Bristol Royal Infirmary. I wheeled into the elevator, the only other person in it being a Chinese man. I had never met him before. He just stared at me and said, "What happened?" Not wanting to encourage a complete stranger to me to ask about intimate details of my life, I said, "What do you mean? I don't understand the question?" I was saying it as if I thought that he was enquiring about something on the ward from which I had just come. Again he said, "What happened?" and continued to stare. Very rude, if you ask me, and by the fifth "What happened?" I just answered, "Hurt my back." He continued to say, "What happened?" I thought that he was a bit freaky and I replied, "Accident. Not very interesting." I was tempted to give him directions to the psychiatric ward or even say, "Well, never mind me. What happened to you, you weirdo? Is the record stuck or something?" Some people. I ask you. Let's put it down to a language or cultural barrier. He was probably born in Bristol, though.

    Even doctors came out with rather untoward comments. A classic was when I started my psychiatry attachment. I met the consultant who would be in charge of me for my time on the psychiatric unit. We had our initial meeting when we talked about what the attachment involved and so forth. He asked what had happened to me. Having told him that I had broken my back, he said something which almost made me speechless. His very words were, "Oh, I knew someone who broke his back. He then fell out of the back of his wheelchair and broke his neck." All that I said was, "Really. How unfortunate. Well, I'll try not to do that."

    Another strange occurrence: I was again in the Bristol Royal Infirmary on a medical attachment. I had bought a sandwich and drink in the hospital charity shop. I sat at one of the tables, after asking a lady if she minded me joining her. Initially, there was no problem. Next, the lady at the table started to tell me all about her husband coming into one of the wards because of "prostrate trouble." I think that she meant prostate. It tends to be a problem only on lying down when it's a prostrate. Best not to try that wisecrack. Then she started to say that I had had a stroke. "You've had a stroke, you've had a stroke." I had had enough of talking about what was wrong with me with people that I didn't know. Instead I tried alternating arms for eating, so that she could see that I had equal strength on both sides. She continued, "You've had a stroke." It began to get quite embarrassing. She probably thought that my speech had been affected due to my silence. I then had to say, "No, I haven't. I hurt my back." At least that turned her voice volume down a bit, but I nonetheless made a swift exit. I swear one day I might be tempted to say, "I broke my back, injured my spinal cord and now I cannot feel or move below my chest level and also, in case you don't know, I cannot go to the toilet like I used to do." That would have probably shut her up; but would it have been worth it? Possibly not. That would get me a bad reputation and it's not really my style. I've not had many weirdos approach me since these few incidents. I don't know why. They seemed to come all at once, too. What was I wearing at the time? What was I doing to encourage this? Now I do sound paranoid. No need, the weirdos have kept their distance……for now.

Chapter 41

Further holidays: viva España in the main

There have been lots of holidays since my accident and in the early stages following my accident I would have never considered it possible for me to have as much freedom as I have been able to gain. Admittedly, there can be restrictions to access, but a lot of limitations are self-imposed. If you are willing to give it a go, then you can visit many places. I can remember meeting someone by chance in Bristol and he had been at the Spinal Injuries Unit when I was there. He had had a lower level back-break than me, but essentially we should have similar abilities as far as wheelchair mobility is concerned. We chatted about how we were getting on. We got on the subject of holidays and I mentioned a few places that I had visited. He looked surprised that I had gone abroad because he had not been abroad at all, expressing worries about the logistics of flying and other things. It was as if he was putting to extremes the safety consciousness taught in hospital. He seemed to have set barriers, which were not really insurmountable. In fact, to me there were no real problems at all, having holidayed abroad a few times. It was certainly easier than I had envisaged before going on my first wheelchair foreign holiday. He was missing out on fantastic times in a warm climate; but who am I to judge? He might not have wanted trips abroad like I did. It did make me think, though, that you can achieve a great deal if you have the will to do so.

So where had I been? Cornwall has already been mentioned. That's hardly abroad, but the accent could fool you occasionally. Where else? Barcelona was the first holiday away with friends. In fact, it was with Andrew and Ellie, who had accompanied on the fateful skiing holiday. Barcelona was a brilliant holiday. We went away in July 1994. Andrew had just passed his medical finals and he was starting work as a doctor proper in the August. Ellie had been qualified for about three years. Had I not had my accident, I would have probably been just about to start work as a doctor. I was two years behind as a result of the accident, but this was not on my mind at all. We were off on a holiday in sunny Spain, my first foreign trip since my accident. It was very exciting, especially the anticipation of my first plane trip in a wheelchair.

The flight over was fine. At the aircraft door, the airport staff lifted me from my own wheelchair into a narrow chair, so that I could be wheeled along the aisle to my seat. Then, when I got level with my seat position, the two men pushing me in this chair lifted me cautiously over the seat arm into the plane seat. My friends had to clamber over me if they needed to relieve themselves during the flight. I had a urosheath and leg-bag on, as I knew that the airplane's toilet was a real impracticability for me on the flight. We were quite excited on the journey over, occasionally saying our pigeon Spanish to each other and in a quiet voice singing Barcelona as sung by Freddie Mercury and a female opera singer whose name escapes me. "Barcelona, what a beautiful horizon," I would sing to Ellie's rebukes of "those aren't the words; it doesn't rhyme." Like an annoying young child, I continued singing it for the rest of the holiday. "Hasta la vista, baby," was our most used expression. We didn't know the Spanish for "I'll be back," though.

We arrived at Barcelona airport. The sky was blue and sun bright through the aircraft window. I had to wait for the other passengers to get off before I did. Then two Spanish men came to lift me from my plane seat to the narrow aisle chair to get me off the plane. I didn't budge. They looked at each other incredulously, as if to say, "He doesn't look that heavy." Then I realised that my seat belt was still on. I couldn't feel the belt preventing their lifting me due to my lack of waistline sensation. Whoops! Pretty amusing, though. Once unrestrained, the Spanish men were a lot more enthusiastic with their lifting than the British had been. I had learnt the words in Spanish for "please lift me slowly," but they were so quick that I didn't get the chance to use the phrase. It was actually far better doing things at a fast pace, although I did feel a little out of control.

We hired a car at the airport. The hotel was in a superb location, just off La Rambla. This is the main central street with lots of bars and general bric-a-brac along it. It leads down to the harbourside. My brother Andrew had been out to Barcelona for the Spanish Formula One Grand Prix a few months before and he had found this very centrally located hotel which had a room adapted for people with disability. It was also pretty cheap for a city hotel. That's, of course, the Ebeneser Wells in me talking. I would even be able to get to the toilet in my hotel room, and so no indignity would be forced on me. My brother had done well for me in his choice of hotel.

We phoned my parents the day that we arrived to let them know that all was okay. I think that this was only fair, in view of the outcome of my last foreign holiday. We had a fantastic holiday this time. Culture was all around with the Dali museum at a town not far from Barcelona, Barcelona cathedral, the unfinished church by Gaudi (Sagrada Familia) and lots more. There was good food and drink and even a pop concert. The pop concert was majorly landing on our feet. We saw adverts for a concert in the Olympic Stadium, which is on a hill that overlooks the city. We went into a record store the morning before the concert and got tickets which cost about fifteen pounds each. And the band was………..Pink Floyd with their famous light and video show. I didn't know many of their songs, other than the ever familiar, "Hey teacher!……." I'll let you sing the rest.

Wow, it was such a good time: a summer evening; a packed stadium; what an atmosphere! Fortunes in life might be changing. When I thought that about two years previously that I was speechless and unsure about whether I could cope out of hospital, it was hard to believe how far I had come. This time I was speechless, but for the right reasons. It was such a good trip. Barcelona was a great city and pretty good for wheelchairs, the Paralympics having been there a few years previously. Dropped kerbs were in abundance. It wasn't perfect for a wheelchair, but in all honesty nowhere is unless I'm living in a dream world. Nothing was insurmountable, though. Lots of good memories and certainly fun outweighed the challenge of this holiday by far. I was beginning to feel like it was possible for me to live a really enjoyable life. I had learned to get by on basic needs in hospital and still have a good life by simply having contact with people that I loved. But, here on holiday, I was enjoying the indulgences of life. It was not essential to the meaning of life, but it did feel good.

Brussels was another memorable trip. It was a long weekend break and I was travelling with Ellie and Andrew again. We were visiting Nick, Ellie's boyfriend, and Nick was in Belgium for a year polishing up his French while doing a Eurocrats sort of thing. He was a barrister trainee at this particular time. The main event for the weekend was a European Ball. It promised to be a really good event.

      I drove up to London where I met Andrew and Ellie and then we went in Andrew's car from London. We were taking the Channel Tunnel, or Chunnel if wanting to save typewriter ink. It had only been open a few months. The Chunnel was good: no sea sickness and very quick and convenient for getting on and off at either end if all went to plan. Shame about the uninspiring views of dark tunnel walls during the journey. We arrived in Belgium in the evening and, having tracked down Nick, we thought that we ought to suss out my hotel as it was getting late. I had tried to be thorough when organising a hotel with wheelchair access. The brochure had said that it was wheelchair accessible and in addition I had faxed the hotel to make sure before booking a room. A return fax stating "wheelchair access, no problem" had been reassuring.

      It was quite a drive out of the city centre, but we did eventually find what seemed to be a far from accessible hotel. How many steps were there at the front? At least fifteen, maybe twenty. We were not perturbed or panicking…..yet. My three companions went into the hotel to see if there were any other entrances and there was a side entrance with only four steps. Andrew and Ellie said that they would take my wheelchair into the hotel to see how accessible things were inside. Nick, our linguist of note, phoned other hotels to check availability while they did this. The hotel owner took them to the elevator because my room was to be a few floors up. The elevator was tiny. It would have been hard to fit a supermodel in it, let alone a two foot wide wheelchair. Apparently Ellie was getting annoyed, motioning that there was no way a wheelchair would fit. The owner grabbed the wheelchair and removed its quick release wheels. In the wheels went and then he folded down the back of the wheelchair frame. In it went. The owner signalled that he had been successful at getting the wheelchair into the elevator. I guess that different people's ideas of wheelchair accessibility vary. By this time, Ellie was having to be controlled by Andrew; usually it's the other way round. They thought that they should look at the room because I could have been carried up the stairs if the worst came to the worst. The bathroom door was very narrow. Need I go on? No. The hotel was completely useless from a wheelchair perspective. Goodness knows how it got labeled "wheelchair accessible" in the holiday brochure. They probably just sent a questionnaire to the hotel owner.

All ended well. In fact, all ended better. We managed to find a wheelchair accessible hotel in a central location. Just two steps at the front and none at a secret side entrance. The room was fine. I got a double room for the price of a single, due to it being a late booking. It was about eleven in the evening by the time we got there. Andrew also got a reduced price for his room in the same hotel. Ellie stayed at Nick's place. Andrew and Nick carefully lifted my bathroom door off its hinges, so that I had more space and easier access to the bathroom. We were set up for a good weekend ahead.

The Ball was starting in the following evening, so we had a day to see a bit of Brussels. We had a lazy time in the morning and afternoon. We had coffee and croissants, pain au chocolat if I dare the pronunciation, and did some aimless wandering about around by our hotel which included some window-shopping. We got a taxi over to the Ball in the evening. It was a black tie and posh frock do. We had already paid for the tickets and everything was inclusive. Luckily, most people spoke English. We were typical Brits abroad. "Excuse me, parlez-vous anglais?" At least, none of us were bad enough to exclaim in a deliberate loud and slow voice, "Do you speak English!" We were given a glass of champagne the moment we arrived. Before I had got to the bottom of the glass, a waiter refilled it. All I had to do was sit and have my champagne infusion. Now I really do sound like a champagne Charlie. Whatever the case, it was like paradise.

Then we were summoned to the dinner table with the sounding of a gong. The menu was in French and I tried to struggle through the ordering process, not understanding much of what was on the menu. Understandably, when my food was served, it was a bit of a mystery as to what I was eating. There was a very pleasant woman in her twenties at our table. For the starter, she asked for just the salad part of it. When I was halfway through my brown chewy mush, I asked her what the menu meant. I wish that I hadn't when I discovered that the first course was duck gullet. It was pretty disgusting, even before I knew what it was. After gambling with my stomach for two more courses, it was back to champagne. Champagne was far safer. Dancing and general drunkenness followed.

I left at about two-in-the-morning in a taxi with Andrew for our hotel. The taxi driver got lost on the way, taking us out of the city by mistake. Initially, I thought that he might be taking us somewhere to cosh us one, but luckily he was just lost. I can remember from the front seat of the taxi asking Andrew at the back, "Do you know what that starter was tonight?" I took much delight in saying, "Duck gullet." Retching and "Disgusting, I ate it all as well, yuck" could be heard as his response, while I creased up laughing.

We finally arrived at the hotel and found our respective rooms. My bathroom light was on. It was a very high-up switch out of my immediate reach and, after finishing in there, I was determined to turn the light off. The light would have been shining into my bedroom, as my door was off its hinges. I'm not a violent person, but for some reason I seemed to be on a mission. I grabbed the towel rail at its non-hinged end and ripped it off in a twisting motion. Then I reached up to the switch, brandishing my towel rail arm extension to turn off the light. After a good sleep, I woke to find another switch lower down which could have equally well turned off the light. Big whoops! To lessen suspicion of being thought of as hooligans, the towel rail was hidden in the drawer and Andrew and Nick lifted the bathroom door back on its hinges. When I first explained to my friends what had happened with the towel rail, they were amazed at how my intoxicated state had taken me over.

The day after the Ball was mainly for recuperation. A morning of rehydration and gradual food reintroduction was followed by a trip to a park in the afternoon. It's almost like recovering from an operation, although the previous night had been much more fun than most of the operations I had had, much as I like the general anaesthetic buzz. Andrew had bought a stunt kite with him, but the wind wasn't very good. Not many stunts were seen; just a disappointed Andrew instead. The evening was spent in central Brussels. We visited the pub that sells the strongest beer in the city and I promise that we hadn't said that morning, "Alcohol, never again." The beer to try was called "Mort Subite" which in translation is "sudden death." It was actually quite tasty, but too rich to have more than a pint or so. Then it was off to the central square. I think that it was called the Grand Place: very busy, whatever it was called.

Next a meal and it was a slightly earlier night in bed when the previous one finally caught up with us.

    A visit to Bruges was enjoyed the following day. A quaint town, well worth a visit. It certainly put my wheelies to the test, what with all the cobbles to negotiate. We then left for home. There was a bit of confusion when getting on the Chunnel at the French end. They would only let our car on the carriage either first or last, because of the wheelchair. This was in case it flooded and they had to evacuate. It made no sense because I couldn't get out of the car when on the carriage, owing to the car door not opening wide enough. So, it shouldn't have mattered where our car was on the carriage. There would not be much hope for survival for anyone else either, if it flooded, fatalist bloke that I am. Try arguing that to a Frenchman. Well, we couldn't. This meant being delayed a couple of hours. It had, nonetheless, been a great break away and the fracas at the Chunnel gave us yet another excuse to slag off the French. Even though I project xenophobia, it's a bit overdone for effect and out of frustration. Give me an attractive woman with a sexy French accent and my xenophobia will go straight out of the window.

    I have also been on several trips with my brother Ali, mainly to Spain. Madrid was a city break. On one of the days that we were there, we had gone to the city centre to look around. Stupidly, I didn't have any pushing gloves with me and it was a bit dirty for wheeling hands. My hands were disgustingly filthy and I really needed to wash them. Our quest was for a toilet and wash basin, and it turned out to be quite some task to find an accessible one. McDonalds was tried. "Ariba, ariba" was exclaimed, as the staff member pointed upstairs. There must be one in the central square, but to my frustration no toilet to be found for my needs. Finally, I saw a waiter in a kitchen area and I pointed to my hands and to the sink to indicate that I needed to use it. He let me go over, only to find that it was a foot-operated tap! It was so apt for how bad things were for wheelchair users there. The waiter did kindly stand on the tap switch, as I washed my hands, though.

    Madrid is an interesting city: a beautiful central park, art museums like the Prada (up thirty steps at the expense of my brother's back, despite help from others), good food and drink. I wrote to the Spinal Injuries Association about the city's difficulties for wheelchair users. I tried to balance the letter by mentioning that, despite the difficulties, Madrid was an interesting place to visit. It got published in the magazine but they edited out the positive side of my letter. It made me look like a really grumpy person, like someone with a real attitude problem, someone who could be labelled as having "spinal cord injury man syndrome." It appeared even worse, when my article was alongside various others saying how great different destinations were. Especially so, when my brother Ali read it in an all-complaining voice imitating Mr Negative. He found it hilarious. I must admit that his impersonation was quite funny.

  The inaccessibility experienced on the visit to Spain didn't put me off. Ali and I went to the Algarve with a day also spent in Seville. It was really good to be enjoying warm holidays on a regular basis. Another holiday, which turned out to be one of the most relaxing ever, was also a Spanish trip. Andrew, my friend from medical school, has a girlfriend whose family owns a farm about a hundred miles from Barcelona. Five of us stayed in one of the farmhouses for a week. We hired a car and stopped off at a supermercado for our food and drink provisions for the holiday. We bought loads and ate and drank like royalty for our time there. It was really hot weather, wonderful food and drink, good company and much relaxation. We were a long distance from any major city or town and we didn't have any distractions like television. We were literally detached from the hustle and bustle of usual life. It was fantastic. I returned home feeling so chilled out. Usually I need a couple of days after a holiday to rest because there has been a certain amount of rushing about on the holiday. This time I felt truly rested and it was a great feeling to have. The holiday had certainly not been a major test. It had been a real pleasure. The traveller in me had indeed returned.

Chapter 42

Outside interests: cinema, fitness and photography

I wasn't just struggling with wheelchair use because I was finding new hobbies as well as returning to medical school and managing to go on occasional holidays. Was there indeed life after spinal cord injury? Golf would never be tried again seriously unless a miracle cure happened. I had played golf to a high standard and my handicap had been six by the time that I was 18 years old. In adapting to my new situation, I had realised that it was impractical to attempt golf from a wheelchair. It would have only led to disappointment and frustration, especially because I had previously been very good at it. It was better for me to consider it a precious relic of my past. "Move on to other things, don't dwell on and cling to past things lost" is probably good advice in this instance. Usually other things can be found to fill the gap in a different way.

  I always enjoyed the cinema, but accessible cinemas were few and far between. The first film that I saw after my accident was Jurassic Park. It was a real treat but quite an effort. My dad took me to a cinema, which has subsequently closed down. I had to hang around suspiciously at some garage entrances while my dad bought the tickets. Eventually, a bloke came out of a secret door with my dad. It was the only way a wheelchair could get into the cinema. Certainly, it was not a conventional route. We came in the front by the cinema screen and my dad helped wheel me up to the top of the slope. I watched the film staying in my wheelchair on the slope. It wasn't the most comfortable viewing position, but that didn't matter because I was seeing a new release feature film at the cinema and it was a good film as well. My dad had made a lot of effort on my behalf to organise this, which was very kind of him. He is a very busy man with his work, but he does still manage to find time for others. Much unspoken respect. Since this visit, I had to search hard for accessible cinemas. There were only a couple in Bristol, which meant that I often didn't have the full choice of films to see. I would have to wait patiently for the desired film to come to a cinema which I could get into.

When the first of the multi-screen cinemas was built in Bristol, my film-watching freedom became seemingly boundless. It was great. I did, however, then get on my disability rights' horse…....or should it be a chair? Whatever the vocabulary used, it makes no difference. My main annoyance was the disabled parking spaces getting filled by cars belonging to able-bodied people. To make matters worse, these less desirable people would park close to my driver's side door, making getting back in my car impossible. This really annoyed me. I would be furious to return to my car to find that I couldn't get in it. Admittedly, there was someone with me at the cinema and they could drive the car out of the space so that the driver's door wasn't blocked enabling me to transfer into the driver's seat. People parking too close to my driver's door would happen despite the message on my driver's side window pleading in capital letters, "PLEASE DO NOT PARK TOO CLOSE. WHEELCHAIR ACCESS NEEDED."

Getting into the car normally was okay because I would get into the driver's seat and then lift the chair frame over me on to the passenger seat after putting the quick-release wheels on the back seat. If ever I was on my own anywhere when the driver's door was blocked, it was a nightmare to get in the car. On those occasions I would have to get in on the passenger side, put the wheelchair wheels on the back seat, fold down the back of the wheelchair and then somehow get the chair frame on to the back seat after lifting it across me. It was a real struggle. I would start swearing out aloud as I did all this and became hotter and hotter and angrier and angrier in the process. When I cooled down, I would finally have to lift my legs from the passenger's side to the driver's side of the car and then lift myself across to the driver side. It was really difficult to do this. I would be fuming by this time. I would stick a suitably rude note on the offending car making my annoyance about the culprit's thoughtless actions apparent.

There were always going to be idiots who didn't appear to have any conception or conscience about parking in disabled parking bays and also too close to cars owned by disabled drivers. Nevertheless, I wanted to try to make the situation at the local cinema change, even though I couldn't change the world. I started writing letters to the cinema company, initially locally and then to head office, explaining my grievances and making suggestions to improve the situation. Each time I wrote, I would get four free tickets. What a bargain! After much writing and free cinema visits, the spaces became better labelled and security staff policed them. So it wasn't all in vain. My pestering had caused action to occur. Then I wrote to complain about the bags to help yourself to Pick 'n Mix sweets being too high for me reach. It was a fair point, but I think that the cinema organisation realised that I had the ulterior motive of free tickets. That letter rightly didn't get a reply. I had pushed my luck too far.

    Sitting in cinema seats watching films wasn't doing much for my fitness. I needed to build up my stamina with regular exercise. Well, at the least I needed to try not to get even less fit. It took absolutely ages for me to get my stamina back. Attending medical college during weekdays was helpful in regaining some fitness because it meant that I had to get out of the house instead of slobbing in bed or in front of television for most of the day. It was also fairly active work, being mainly on the wards. In addition to this, I would go for long pushes in my spare time. There is a promenade by Clevedon seafront of about two miles from one end to the other and back again. It is flat, in the sense that there are no steps or obstacles over the distance, but it does have steep slopes along its path. There are also fantastic views over to South Wales to be enjoyed on a clear day. It was an ideal push to build up my fitness and I would time myself completing it to add a bit of competition to each visit. I used to go there quite frequently. Even though fitness was the principal reason for going, a crane game device in which toys can be fished out if lucky gave a distraction from the trip being purely focused on regaining fitness. Many twenty pence pieces of mine filled the wretched crane machine and very occasionally I would succeed and return home with a furry companion.

    As my fitness improved, I was even thinking of doing a wheelchair marathon at one stage. Let's call it marathon madness, fortunately a temporary condition in my case. It affected me so much that I even contacted the organisers of the London Marathon. In order to enter the London one as a wheelchair contestant, you needed to have done a marathon already in something like under four hours.

Instead I could have entered the Great North Run, Push or whatever it's called, which I believe is a half-marathon. Eventually, the cost of a racing chair put me off. Well, that's my convenient excuse in any case. Despite not entering an official marathon, I must have gone mad one weekend when I did the Clevedon seafront push fourteen times in my standard wheelchair. So I suppose that I have done a marathon, but a staged one……in about thirty hours. Now I only go up to the seafront if I'm desperate for sea air or fancy a Mr Whippy ice cream: far more pleasure, lots less pain. Wisdom indeed comes with time and experience.

 My main exercise outside work comes from swimming. Soon after my tracheostomy tube was removed, a trip to the Spinal Injuries Unit in Salisbury enabled me to give it a go. This was with the security of having a physiotherapist in the pool with me. Even so, it was quite nerve-wracking to get into a swimming pool knowing that I couldn't move my legs. The fear of drowning was firmly in my consciousness when I felt so physically powerless. I felt a bit like a child again, having to be coaxed into the pool. Nonetheless, this supervised swimming session was a success in that it gave me enough confidence to go to my local swimming pool. Initially I went with a friend, just in case I started to sink or panic halfway across the pool. Soon I could manage on my own. Nowadays it's quite a regular thing for me to do. I try to go at least once a week.

 It is fantastic to exercise out of the wheelchair. I feel so much freedom being in the water and escaping the metal prison of my chair. It's an amazing release from these endless shackles and reminders of immobility. I also feel so much better physically after a swim. My leg stiffness and spasms improve, my chest is less painful and my mind feels much clearer. I didn't get the opportunity to do swimming when I was in hospital because of my inconvenient tracheostomy tube. The reconstruction operation on my throat not only gave me speech again and left me without the hassle of caring for the tracheostomy tube; it also meant that I could go swimming. It has enabled me to go back to work, communicate freely and have a hobby which is one of my most valued. Swimming is really more than a hobby. It makes me feel so much more healthy. A prescription of regular swimming does much more than any medication could do.

Each time I go, I have to change clothes while in my chair. This is a real skill and it's a test of endurance in itself. I have to lift my bottom off the chair with my hands doing a push up on the wheels. Simultaneously, I use one hand to pull at my trousers or trunks. After several tugs, my garments are either on or off depending on whether I want to be dressed or undressed. I have got used to it now, but initially it was very tiring. I used to be wetter with perspiration from the effort of changing than with water from swimming.

Some people have been interesting in how I get from my wheelchair to the pool thinking that I might just be tipped in from my wheelchair. That sounds like fun but it's not how it's done. Firstly, I get near to the poolside and then lower myself down from my chair on to a swim mat strategically placed on the floor, the mat being there for protection in case my descent from the wheelchair is less controlled and more rapid than planned. A reason for learning the chair-floor transfer in hospital has now become apparent to me. Then, sat on my bottom with my legs out in front, I move to the pool's edge using my arms as my propellant. Last of all, once my legs are in the water, I do a forward diving motion into the water. Swimming can at last begin. My legs dangle low and powerless and I wear socks to protect my feet from being scratched when they hit the bottom of the pool. I am some sight to behold!

I can only manage breaststroke in standard fashion and a modified backstroke with my arms at my side rather than swinging past my ears. I am a little slow with old folk going almost double my pace, but I need to set my own goals and ignore others. We are all different and I think that I have a good reason for being slower than others. First of all I would only do widths of the pool, but now I have settled to doing twenty lengths at each visit. There is indeed measurable progress. Now I even do widths underwater. In fact, it's a lot quicker swimming on the bottom of the pool because my legs aren't able to dangle and slow me down. Getting out of the pool used to be difficult with no leg power to push me out, but now my technique has improved such that I don't even think about it. It is remarkable progress, often only appreciated by actively looking back on things.

Photography was a new hobby for me. I had been bought a camera with lots of features that I didn't have a clue about. It also had some idiot modes on it, which were the only ones that I could use, but I thought that it would be good and maybe even fun to learn how to use the other functions. This attracted me to a photography course advertised in the Local Education Authority booklet of courses. It was cheap to enrol and it happened once a week in the evening over a period of ten weeks. It was ideal to fit in after work at medical college and the course was held conveniently in accessible school buildings a couple of miles from home. I seized the opportunity but also felt anxious that I could look a bit of a silly tit with my lack of photography knowledge. The course was for pretty inexperienced photographers, though, and these worries turned out only to be beginner's jitters. I had to do a project of producing a portfolio of ten photographs. Mine was on the subject "From the cradle to the grave." My niece was a subject at one end of the spectrum and my dad laughed when he was at the other end together with a gravestone at the village church.

I got through the course and I now put to good use what I learned on it. It's good fun to prepare mounts and to frame your own photos. In fact, I have got some that I did since the course on the walls of my cottage. It's a personalised and hopefully not too egotistical way of decorating my house. They can also make good gifts. Perhaps I'll set up a business. I don't think so. The good thing about photography is that I can pick a camera up whenever I like and don't have to keep practising at it. I have probably insulted hundreds of photographers now with my naïve oversimplification. Sorry, I'm certainly not an expert and surely what matters is what I get out of it, so my insults will continue. All in all, the course had been a really good thing to do.

I seemed to be building a life again. I had my independence, hobbies, friends and studies. I was going on holiday as much as most other people and having a really good time. Admittedly, my impairments were circumscribing some of my choices, but I was not missing out on a great deal. I was realistically attempting to develop the career that I had originally set out to follow. If all went well, I might have a more full and interesting life than many other people who are unaffected by spinal cord injury. I never knew how I would adapt to paralysis. Had I been asked about it before I was injured, I would have probably been far more pessimistic than I am now. It made me think that whoever says that they would rather die than be paralysed probably only imagines the worst and is most likely wrong in what they think it will be like. You only know how you will truly cope with something when you are there experiencing it.

Chapter 43

Philadelphia: the pain was not mine this time

At the beginning of the final year of medical school was the medical elective. It is when you have the opportunity to go anywhere in the world for up to ten weeks to see medicine practised. This was to be one of the highlights of my training. I chose Philadelphia and I registered on a four week pain management course at Jefferson Medical Centre….or maybe I should spell it Center to convey American loyalty.

    I was to spend the autumn of 1995 there. I was going to see "Philly in the fall" as the Americans used to call it when I was there. I had just passed my written final examinations after a lot of work and it was very exciting to be off to America for about two months. It almost seemed like a reward for my efforts and it was great to be anticipating a trip where the emphasis was not solely on work. Admittedly, it was interesting to see and learn a bit of medicine, but the main emphasis was on enjoying myself. An elective report had to be written within a few months of its completion, but this was all that was expected. So it was skyscrapers and Amish country that would welcome me and I was very excited.

    It was going to be a long time away from my secure home base with all its conveniences. I travelled over with my parents and they stuck around for the first couple of weeks which was really helpful as I settled in. My accommodation was basic but near my room there was an accessible toilet and shower….or is that a restroom, man? Importantly, I could get to the toilet, often not having that privilege when visiting foreign places. Soon I would get used to some of the American lingo. Being a non-smoker, at least I didn't have to worry about saying that I was dying for a fag when asking for a cigarette and then being directed to the YMCA or worse.

    The hospital and pain clinic where I would spend much of my working day was about ten minutes away by wheelchair or on foot, whichever you chose to use. This was really convenient and I would enjoy an early morning stroll to work each day to wake me up. It was much better than sitting impatiently in a car as part of a traffic queue for thirty or so minutes. My dad knew a radiologist who was based in the X-ray department at the Philadelphia hospital and I was going to spend a couple of weeks in this department after I finished my pain management course. This friend of my father's was very pleasant and helpful. I, my parents, he, his wife and son met up on a couple of occasions during my time there. They were very welcoming. One night we went to a spaghetti opera restaurant where the waiters and waitresses have a burst of singing at interludes in the meal: good fun indeed. It was a brilliant city to visit and having people to tell me where to go was very helpful and gladly that was the informative "tell you where to go" rather than the angry abusive one.

Was the work interesting? I naturally had an interest in pain management having been part of the system in the UK as a patient already. It was a really valuable four weeks, even if there were early starts: seven o'clock to be exact. The American doctors were really enthusiastic, so much so that it was almost infectious. Their desire for knowledge and to educate others was amazing. They would often bring in articles for me, saying why they were interesting. One day, though, I knew that I couldn't get quite as excited as some of them. One of the doctors said that there were talks worth attending at 6-15 each morning. Initially I thought that she was joking and fortunately I controlled myself expressing amazed disbelief. My sleep was too precious and, had I gone to these talks, I would have truly been losing the plot. Having not made my feelings known, I nodded in subdued interest to the doctor's suggestion. My elective was not to be all about work, after all. It was good, though, to have dynamic and interested people around to inspire me in my pursuit for knowledge.

I met the Head of the Pain Department on the first morning. He said that they couldn't recall having had medical students on the course and that I was probably the first. After explaining the different things that went on, he said that I was free to choose what I wanted to do each day depending on what interested me. There was no rigid timetable. What a result it was for me. I could even go off sightseeing on some days if I wanted. My time there was about getting the most out of my trip, both in work and leisure. It was refreshing not to have an ogre breathing down my neck. I would be attending the hospital because I enjoyed it. The fact that I turned up on most days of the four-week course is testament to how good it was. However, I didn't go to excesses in my enthusiasm because I would rarely finish late in the day; quite rightly after the early starts! I didn't mind getting up early, though, when I could often finish in the early afternoon and enjoy a bit of Philadelphia.

I did learn a lot about pain management. There were some memorable patients. One in particular sticks in my mind. I found the case quite upsetting and frustrating when people might think that I had enough to contend with in my own situation. I'm not hysterically upset about my own circumstances and I'm not much into self-pity in any case. My circumstances might even make some patient situations experienced seem more saddening. The patient who stays in my memory was a man in his early-twenties. He attended with his older sister. He had damaged his arm nerve supply in an accident involving a window-frame falling on his shoulder. I can't remember all the details of the accident. There was no obvious outward problem on initially meeting him until he was assessed in more detail in the clinic room where I was an observer. The doctor chatted with him about what was wrong and the young man mentioned how his neck had a lot of strain on it as a result of his problem. The young man seemed desperate to have something done.

The doctor approached to examine him. He touched the affected arm. The whole arm went into terrible spasm motions. The young man had no control over it and his neck was shoved to one side. He made groaning noises in response to this demon, as he waited for it to subside. He looked really shaken when it finished, almost as if he had been in a fist fight. While all this took place, his sister had to cover her face and shut her eyes in pained anguish, unable to watch her brother's terrible ordeal and the situation in which he found himself. It was a desperate situation. The patient almost pleaded for something to be done. "Can't you just cut the nerves? I don't mind not being able to move my arm. It's just that my neck and other things are really affected by all this jerking." The doctor explained that cutting the nerves would not help the situation and that the jerking was in fact due to damaged nerves. There was medication that could be tried but in the main it was a difficult condition to treat. It was so frustrating. Here was a young man who had his life devastated by a terribly unfortunate act of fate. What drove home how very sad the situation was how upset his sister appeared as she covered her distressed face with her hand. What mental suffering. And what was the point of it all? On the surface, this man appeared normal. Behind the clinic curtains lay someone with a very limiting condition. He had to cope with a lot more than the average Hank the Yank. This terrible condition probably affected so many others besides the patient as well. In many ways, although not exactly the same, some aspects of this case could parallel what had happened to me. Certainly, it reminded me of the implications of my accident for my circle of friends and family.

There were many patients attending the clinic who outwardly looked fine. They did not have wheelchairs or other visible signs of difficulty. Behind the clinic doors, though, many of them were dreadfully disabled by pain syndromes. Some were not at all independent. Behind their curtains lay turmoil and distress which the doctor had to understand and attempt to alleviate to some degree in some fashion. What mattered was the fact that these people had lives which were extremely limited. The Head of the Department gave a metaphor for what he tries to do for these patients when they attend. He pictures himself and the patient at the entrance to a dark tunnel. He and the patient have to attempt to get to the other side of the tunnel in some way or other. They try different routes together. Hopefully they end up on the other side of tunnel after trying these different routes. On the other side of the tunnel is rarely someone who is pain-free. The doctor hopes that on the other side is a person better adapted to their pain syndrome and able to live in a more fulfilling way. The different routes tried are the different treatments tried for the pain, the doctor and patient being partners in their quest for a solution. With this approach, at least someone has tried to help the patient. This path through the tunnel requires mutual trust. Mutual trust is an essential part of good doctor-patient partnership. Sadly, there tend to be no fast cures and cure in many scenarios often means adaptation to the situation rather than symptom relief. I did indeed learn a lot, both about medical treatments and about relating to patients. Despite having an insight into the patient perspective through my own circumstances, there is still a lot for me to learn. It does some good to feel humble and challenged occasionally.

So what did Philadelphia have to offer? Now I'll be the American travel agent. Wow, what a city! There are sights galore, man. The Liberty Bell, Independence Hall, various museums, Amish country a car drive away and much more. Also, there are so many interesting places nearby. New York, Atlantic City, Washington DC and Boston are to name a few. Philadelphia has much more, too, with lots of really good restaurants and places to go out to after a day at the hospital. The city has got a good feel to it. I had picked well when choosing a place to visit for the elective. It was also an interesting time to be out there because the O J Simpson trial was going on. The buzz about the city on the lunchtime that his "not guilty" verdict was announced was truly enthralling. It was on the radio and television everywhere. Everyone was talking about it and people's reactions added to the atmosphere. It was certainly a memorable time.

Aside from this drama, who visited me? I wasn't inundated with visitors. Well, in actual fact, apart from my parents, it was only my brother Ali who came from the English side of the pond to visit. Let the truth be known: I'm Norman no mates! It was really good to see my brother. He had a terrible trip over with a bit of a bad tummy on the plane. He's an airline pilot, so it must have been a bug rather than airsickness and for the first few days he was confined to bed. He was the patient this time. I would go off to a day's work at the hospital and see him later in the day. I would fetch him drinks and so forth from the supermarket and he certainly wasn't putting it on. He seemed to be suffering and genuinely needed some sympathy, even though I was only around after a day's work to give it.

When he recovered his normality, we planned a trip to New York for a weekend. It was really hard to find a hotel in the centre of New York, and so we ended up staying on the city's outskirts. This didn't greatly matter, since we were hiring a car for the trip in any case. We had both been to New York on a family holiday about fifteen years previously. New York is a very exciting city. We managed to do a lot in the weekend and rather bizarrely the wheelchair probably helped speed things up. We planned to see the Empire State Building, the Twin Towers, Statue of Liberty and Ellis Island, but didn't know whether we would achieve this in our limited time there. There were massive queues when we arrived at all these attractions. Being in a wheelchair meant that we were taken to the front of the queue or to a secret lift……or elevator if being truly American. It was probably overdoing the rights for disabled bit, but we were in a hurry……and, since they insisted, we weren't going to argue. So, if anyone wants to do a whistle stop tour of New York, I've got a spare wheelchair; at a charge of course!

It was brilliant to arrive at a tourist attraction and to be escorted to the front of the queue. At least it was some payback for all the other hassles that result from wheelchair use. Just getting out of bed and going to the toilet is a trial compared to what it used to be like, so it was good to make up for it by having preferential treatment when sightseeing. It was a very memorable trip and those skyscrapers are unbelievably high. The lifts are necessarily fast, too. As we went up in one of the Twin Towers' elevators, the floors would increase five at a time on the electronic display in the lift. The views of the city were fantastic once at the top, seen in the gaps between the passing clouds. We spotted the Statue of Liberty and Ellis Island, sights to be visited later in the day and appearing quite small from such a height. The boat trips necessary to visit those places were fun, although helpers made a good attempt at tipping me out of my wheelchair backwards when boarding the boat. My brother Ali, fortunately ever vigilant, caught me and my wheelchair from behind as I came off the steep ramp into the boat. This prevented a nasty headache or worse. Sadly, you can't trust enthusiastic volunteers to do it how it should be done. That's the thing about being in a wheelchair in those sorts of situations. You lose so much control and often rely on other people listening to your instructions. Sometimes people are just so intent and in such a rush to help that they don't listen. Usually the person in the wheelchair knows how it is done best. It can be a tricky situation: you are grateful to have help, while at the same time far from grateful to be tipped out of the wheelchair. C'est la vie. What can you do? Bravo alpha.

Before I got on the boat, we had to wait for a lady wheelchair user coming off it. She walked down a few steps from the boat, as her wheelchair was pushed down a steepish slope. She was grossly overweight and at the bottom of the steps was extremely breathless. I think that she was in a wheelchair simply because of her size. I had feelings of how dreadful it was for her. Here's me making assumptions. Here's me judging her situation and I didn't know her from Adam, or Eve for that matter. She might have been a very happy lady. My feelings were of shock and disbelief, yet I was only too aware not to make assumptions about her. It reminded me that I as much as anyone else have prejudices that need to be constantly challenged by myself. Otherwise I might become a nasty person without knowing it. Importantly, on this occasion I shouldn't make my shock apparent and certainly not whisper my surprise to my brother in front of her. From what I remember, I think that we only shared our disbelief later. After all, everyone has feelings whether fat, thin, ugly, disfigured or any other feature that encourages people's prejudice. And what shouldn't be forgotten is that beauty is in the eye of the beholder; so who am I to talk? The boat trip was well worth it. The Statue of Liberty was good to get up close to and it was interesting to learn when on Ellis Island about the ancestry of different settlers in America. It's strange, though, how people seen or met are often just as memorable as the places themselves.

    The visit to New York didn't all go well. We managed to get a parking ticket despite displaying my orange disabled parking badges in the hire car windscreen. They were not the usual accepted badges for New York. That was probably why when we returned from lunch at a "Pret à Manger" café that there was the unappreciated gift of a fifty dollar parking violation invoice. We had been really "Ready to Eat" when we had finally got to lunch, having been at pains to find a suitable parking place. These pains had been in vain because now our wallets would feel a bit of pain. Ali was furious and I was a little annoyed, too, but ready to forget about it and get on with the rest of the day. After all, it was only a small amount compared to the cost of the whole trip, not that I make a habit of accruing parking tickets. It's boring to dwell on. We were in Yankland to "have a gas," to have fun and not to moan over unwelcome tickets. Philadelphia beckoned again after what seemed a brief time away, but we had seen and done so much in a couple of days. Plenty of ticks for the "I've done this" book if you're that sort of person. New York is a great place and at least being shot or mugged hadn't been added to the tick book.

    Then there was a visit to Philadelphia zoo which was fun, although not much different to most other zoos that I have visited. I went there with my parents. My lasting memory of that day was of my dad stopping for petrol on the journey back and of him having to pay for it before the petrol attendant would put fuel in the tank. Quite bizarre, but apparently people had been known to drive off without paying which explained the paying before getting the fuel routine. And I must say that my dad, grey haired Professor Wells in half-moon glasses, must have looked like a real dead ringer for a rough diamond in disguise.

Another trip was to Atlantic City for the day. This was again with the old folk, my mum and dad. We set our gambling limit before we left and managed to get through this fairly quickly. After a while the clatter of machines and coins was a bit of a headache. "Now who's the old folk?" I hear you say. Then a walk or in my case a wheel along the boardwalk was a must. Maybe I should have sung an alternative song while doing so. "Down by the boardwheel." No, it wouldn't catch on.

I did meet a few people when over in the States. One was a man in a wheelchair who had just started work as a doctor at the hospital in which I was based. He was very friendly and invited me out with some of his friends, mainly medical staff, on a couple of occasions. He had also had a spinal cord injury and he had been injured some years before me. It was heartening, though, for me to see someone in a similar situation to mine who was actually working as a doctor without any obvious problems. This lay ahead for me and I was still unsure as to whether I could make the transition from medical student to doctor. Nevertheless, my confidence in my future work capabilities had been enhanced by seeing him manage to do his job.

On a night out, one of his friends asked me what I missed about England. It was difficult to think of anything in particular. Pubs and my own bed were the top two, but my own bed probably doesn't qualify as typically English. I was not away long enough to miss people very much and I had also brought half of my close family with me. It was good to be meeting new people, too. I am sure that had I been away for longer and on my own that friends and family would have topped the list of things missed. Despite my loyalty to England, there are plenty of reasons to return to America and many good memories. The trip as a whole was a real success. I was so inspired by it that I won a prize for my elective report. In fact, I may have even made a profit from the trip by having managed to get money from charitable trusts as a result of begging letters written beforehand. I don't think that I could live in America long-term, but it certainly has enough charm to attract me back and the American people that I met came across as very friendly and polite. I have often heard people complain about how Americans continually wish you to have a nice day, but I would certainly rather they wish me to have a nice day than have them ignore me. I wasn't going to analyse whether or not people were being false. They were just being friendly and it makes you feel good to have friendly people around you. I can remember the checkout assistant at a shop in Heathrow airport on my return from America. Sniffling her nose, she brusquely asked for my money, no smile or eye contact. I knew plainly that I had returned to England. People certainly interacted less back home.

  The whole attitude of Americans to disabled people was different as well. They would put themselves out to make things as equal as possible for disabled people and the main thing about it all was their positive attitude. Admittedly, they have more laws for disabled rights than Britain does, but laws do not always lead to action. They still need to be enforced. The willingness to help people with impairments seemed far more forthcoming in America. I sensed this very much when there. I felt like a person whose rights were considered as important, rather than as a nuisance in a wheelchair. They did not believe in inequality. I'm pretty sure that in Britain we don't believe in it, too, but we often do nothing about it. The Americans seemed to put more into effect. They were far more proactive. Even though I am giving American admiration, there was one thing that I found absurdly amusing when there. It was the disabled toilets. They were in abundance in America. Where am I going with this? Don't worry, toilets aren't a secret perversion of mine despite my frequent ramblings. Most of the disabled toilets had a wide door, but what a shame that in many of them the door opened inwards preventing me shutting it behind me. I guess that their hearts were in the right place at least. All in all, America had been a good place to visit. God bless America.

Chapter 44

What a weekend! My left foot, casualty and imminent medical exams

Let me set the scene. It was June 1996 and I had been preparing for a few months for my final medical exams. The exams were going to be over a week and a half in June. If successful, I would be allowed to start work as a doctor at the beginning of August. If unsuccessful, I would have to redo them in November and delay working by at least four months. Understandably, there was a lot of importance attached to them. The exams mainly involved examining patients and viva examinations, and so were quite stressful.

It was the weekend before the exams started and the first exam was on the Monday. My left foot had become a bit more swollen on the Friday before this weekend. Then it suddenly became very red and swollen on the Saturday. I had to get the foot seen to and I couldn't go to my general practitioner because it was Saturday night. I had to go to the accident and emergency department in central Bristol. What a complete nightmare. Off I went at about nine o' clock with my dad accompanying me along with my pathology lecture notes.

A couple of my friends from London medical school were working as doctors in the accident department but, of course, they weren't on duty. My dad and I waited patiently in the waiting area, having explained my problem to the woman at the reception desk. It was truly a saga. We sat there as different characters entered the same area. There were people with stab injuries, drunk and generally abusive people, and then people with less obvious problems. We tried to look as inconspicuous as possible, since we didn't want any rage directed our way. "Why me? Another story for my catalogue," I thought to myself.

After an hour or so, we were ushered into the main accident area. My dad and I sat in one of the examination cubicles. There were a couple of doctors in the department who I knew from a recent medical attachment I had done. They asked what was the matter out of fascinated interest, while I waited for the doctor delegated to see me. I pointed dejectedly to the offending foot. Having at last been seen by one of the accident and emergency doctors, I had a foot X-ray and some blood tests done. The diagnoses going through my head were a fracture, a leg vein blood clot and infection of the skin, also known as cellulitis.

  I was accommodated under the orthopaedic doctors' care. These are the doctors who deal with fractures, bones and the like. No fracture was seen on my X-ray. Even so, I could have knocked my foot and sprained it without knowing, since I couldn't feel pain there due to my paralysis. They seemed to think that I most likely had cellulitis, though. I had broken skin between my toes, athlete's foot in other words. Don't you dare take the Michael. I know that I'm not an athlete, so don't rub it in. Whatever the words, bugs getting through cracks in the skin of my foot was how I probably got the cellulitis. I had to stay in hospital overnight and for most of Sunday to have antibiotics given into my bloodstream. The orthopaedic junior doctor tried to lessen my stress with an amusing joke when he assessed me late on the Saturday night. "What's the difference between an orthopaedic surgeon and a carpenter? A carpenter knows the name of two antibiotics." It did make me chuckle, especially as it mocked his bosses. It also momentarily got my mind away from the reams of pathology notes.

  After explaining the imminence of my exams when seen on the Sunday morning ward round, they kindly let me home with some antibiotic tablets later that day. I escaped hospital just in time for my exams the following week. All I remember of the exams was going into the hospital to do them and then having to rush home to elevate my swollen foot. It's bad enough doing these exams from a wheelchair without the added burden that had been thrown my way. Even though I had been delighted to attend the exams in view of my foot's condition the fateful weekend before, it was even better to finish them. There was a wait of two weeks before the results came out and, having done the exams, it was a time to relax before knowing the results. I appreciated having this free time whatever happened, even if my temperament was slightly offset and subdued from the anticipation of what the results would be like. If I passed, it would be a month before work started.

Chapter 45

Results of finals: dad had to do the deed

The exam results were going to be displayed on a noticeboard in Senate House, a university building inaccessible to wheelchairs. My dad had to go there for me to find out the outcome of my efforts. I was very nervous about it all and didn't know how best he should tell me. Bad news is usually better delivered in person. The day came when they were going to be on view. How about my poor dad rather than just me? We were literally in this together. He had another stressful task to do on my part. He's a hardy man, though, and has been very good at empathising when times have been bad. Things weren't necessarily going to be bad, though. I think that this is one of the few times when it's best to be pessimistic. Then there's less of a distance to fall from if all goes pear-shaped. However, it's only good to be privately pessimistic rather than publicising pessimism to fellow candidates. There's no one more sickening than a person who has passed with flying colours after they have gone around saying to everyone how badly they have done. This sickening feeling is especially so for those who fail. It was really difficult to know how I had performed because they were practical exams. None of them had gone disastrously, but that was all I could tell.

It was midmorning and I was at home. The phone rang. It was dad. Always one to keep me in suspense, he said, "I've been into Senate House to get your results." Next came, "I've got some good and some slightly less good news............You haven't got any distinctions, but the good news is that you passed." Who gave a damn about distinctions? I had finished the medical course and the medical degree was now mine. What an immense relief. What a true delight. It had been hard work, but I had had invaluable support from those close to me. Naturally, all those people were delighted, too. It was partly their success in my eyes. Paid work as a doctor started in about a month. Now I could really enjoy a month's well-earned rest. Another chapter in my life had been completed and an exciting new one was about to start.

Chapter 46

August 1996: transition from student to actual doctor

My work as a doctor was to start at Frenchay Hospital, the place of some of my previous adventures. This time I was the doctor, though. I had achieved the title of doctor after a lot of toil. Now I had to see whether I could live up to the stresses of the job rather than just clinging to the doctor label. The Regional Postgraduate Medical Dean had met me about a year previously to organise a work package for me, so that I could work relatively close to home. I was going to be funded through his budget and my job was as a supernumerary. In other words, I was an additional pair of hands to the standard medical team. This did not, however, mean an easy life. Hospital work can be so very hectic and my job was still going to be busy. Also, the transition from being a protected medical student to being a doctor with far more responsibility is a big one for anyone who is newly qualified. Every doctor starting work for the first time is initially nervous. It did make a big difference, though, to have a job tailored to my needs. I had thought that I might have to fight to get a job and possibly might even be discriminated against. However, this had been prevented from happening by having had the Postgraduate Medical Dean's involvement at an opportune stage. What a pleasant relief.

As it turned out, I worked much the same as any other doctor. Practical procedures were tried under supervision of the more senior doctors in the team. Experience takes a while to gain. I could already take blood and put in cannulas for drips, although this improved greatly with practice. More tricky procedures such as chest drain placement, lumbar punctures and central vein line placement were possible after a lot of perseverance. Now I am competent in these techniques, I am grateful to the patients and my teachers for their patience. My learning of these skills was really no different to any other doctor. I have had to be more conscious when doing practical procedures of where to position myself, the patient and the equipment. Even when I examine a patient, I need to develop alternative strategies to make proficient examination possible. For a start, the patient needs to move closer to the edge of the bed, so that I can reach them adequately. I can manage without them doing this, but it is just more difficult.

It's strange how you gain confidence as a doctor. I can look back after five years of work and see how I have progressed. Now, I no longer need to be a doctor tagged on to the team. Nonetheless, it was extremely valuable to have had my first three to four years funded as a supernumerary while I gained my competency as a hospital practitioner. I feel very privileged to have been given this opportunity by the Regional Postgraduate Medical Dean. It seems to have made sense for everyone, though. Everyone has gained something. I can now be a productive part of the National Health Service machinery, not that I wasn't this from the start. On this occasion, the NHS has not lost yet another doctor after investing a sizable financial sum into his training.

My jobs have been mainly in the South West of England. All the hospitals in which I have worked have been okay. It's never perfect because there are always things that could be better. But if working conditions are manageable without too much hassle, then it's fine with me. I can remember checking out hospitals for their suitability. I basically looked at hospital layout, ward layout, commuting distance from home, doctors' mess and accommodation, and canteen facilities. There was certainly more preparation needed on my part than the average person would have to make. Planning was the key and although it couldn't solve everything, it certainly made things feel a lot easier when done properly. It gave me some sense of control of the situation.

A new stage of my life had been reached. I was now a doctor having found that I could manage what being a doctor entailed. It was a significant step. It was like when I returned home from hospital, like when I went on a foreign holiday for the first time since my accident and like when I started back at medical school. I had felt life's unfairness when reflecting on the past at certain stages, realising my vulnerability to life's wounds but also feeling so good inside when things were achieved. My attitudes to people's capabilities had been widened by my own experiences. Goodness knows what my next significant step would be. A song by Shawn

Colvin called "New Thing Now" echoes some sentiments felt. I had had everything exposed in my ordeal and after this it had been good to get back home again, then return to medical school and now to be working as a doctor. I have been very aware that each stage had been a new thing at the time and that it could go wrong. To move on with challenges is always a gamble. Whatever challenge came my way next, I hoped that I would not lose my optimism in the human spirit. If I lost my house, job or anything that had been moulded as important to me, I prayed to keep my will to continue plugging away at this life. It was who I was and the people who mattered to me that had far more importance than a job, house or bank balance. Nevertheless, my career did feel good and gave me a lot of satisfaction.

Chapter 47

Further medical exams

Could I believe that I was here? When I anticipated doing postgraduate medical exams, I had already done over a year of work as a doctor. If I wanted to progress beyond a certain level in hospital medicine, I had to get further qualifications. People find it especially hard because the exams have to be taken at the same time as doing busy hospital jobs. The MRCP, Membership of the Royal College of Physicians, was the qualification that I needed. It was in two parts and the two parts typically had about a year or so between them.

The first part was a multiple choice exam. The second part was an exam in two stages about six weeks apart, the first stage being a written exam involving medical case problem solving, data interpretation and photos to muse over. The second stage consisted of a clinical exam in which patients had to be examined in front of examiners, so-called short cases. There was also a longer case and a viva. If I passed the exam, I gained Membership of the Royal College of Physicians. It's no easy feat to achieve for even a severely able-bodied person, let alone someone with as large a physical impairment as myself. Usually only a third of the candidates pass the exam at each sitting, so it is indeed very hard and a major accomplishment for anyone who gets it. Well, after getting part one on the first attempt in January 1998, it took me three goes to get through the written stage of part two. Then, all that was in my way of the qualification was the second stage of part two, the clinical exam.

I can remember the clinical exam very well. The University Hospital of Wales in Cardiff was where it was held. My slot for the exam was early in the day and I drove with plenty of time to spare because I didn't know exactly where to go and to park. I managed to find a car park in the hospital grounds very near the part of the hospital in which the exam was to take place. I even had to pay for my parking, despite having orange badges identifying a disabled driver. I wondered whether this was a bad omen for the day ahead. I sat in the car with over an hour to kill. It was like before a driving test with all the nerves that I felt. After suppressing my anxiety for as long as I could, I went into the hospital and bought a coffee for a caffeine fix. At least I don't smoke for nerves. It wouldn't have made a good impression with the examiners if I had smelt like fag-ash Lil (or perhaps it should be Bill). I find it so valuable to relax in my own quiet way before a major test such as a really important exam, rather than having many other nervous people around distracting me. With about quarter of an hour to go, I ventured to where the candidates anxiously sit together. We lined up in trios and then got escorted off in turn to different examiners. Time went by quickly once in the exam and it was over before I knew it.

 Thank goodness to have done the exam whatever the outcome might be. I didn't find out the result for a few weeks, but the outcome turned out to be good. I had passed and it was a fantastic feeling of achievement. It was October 1999 by this time and I had negotiated another obstacle. This was a very important obstacle for my career progression and it was in fact one that a couple of years previously that I thought not possible without dispensations made for my disability. I had done it, though, and had surprised myself by doing so.

 Here comes the amateur philosophy, so go to the start of the next chapter if you want to skip it. Set no boundaries to what can be achieved. Have faith in yourself and it is possible to achieve astounding things. I probably did this and have surprised many people including myself. I didn't think this so much at the time, but on looking back it is pretty astonishing in view of so much. Just remember where I was just a few years before: in a hospital bed, speechless and anxious about mobilising in a wheelchair. My impairment of not being able to feel or move below my chest had not prevented me from successfully completing a challenging exam in which the technique of examining patients needs to be very polished and accomplished. That's enough of my self-praise. It was merely a means to an end, rather than to impress other people. I needed to get this exam in order to progress as a hospital doctor. If my achievements and situation have shaped people's attitudes in a positive manner, though, it's all the better.

 What next can I achieve, professionally or other? Who knows? I certainly don't, but I do have a lot of faith in life being okay whatever happens. I have done far more than I ever thought possible and enjoyed it, too, despite the odd nervous moment. It makes me more optimistic than ever. Life had dealt me good and bad blows and I have come through the bad ones, however uncertain life has looked. There is so much wonder to come from it all. Life is great. Put your mind to it and achieve more than you ever imagined possible. It's all to do with your approach to life. Take things day by day, whatever may come your way, and try not to be filled with dismay. If that turns out to be a recognised cliché, I will truly crack up in uncontrollable laughter.

Chapter 48

A voyage to remember: sun, calm sea, sea urchin spikes, two Norwegians and a broken front wheel

There's not much philosophy in this chapter, just lots of fun. It was without question a brilliant holiday. The location was the Canaries, the holiday was aboard a Sailor Training Ship called the Lord Nelson, the time was February 1998 and the weather was glorious for the time of year. It was fantastic to be in a place where every morning would greet me with a clear blue sky, in the knowledge that back home it was definitely cold and half-certain to be wet. I had never been away on holiday in a warm climate during the cold months of England. I hear the miserable Englishman say, "What bloody months aren't cold in England anyway?"

The ship was adapted to accommodate people with physical impairments, as well as those without. There were ten permanent crew who knew what they were doing when it came to sailing. The paying passengers amounted to about forty in number and about ten were disabled. This collection of people had varying sailing experience and some had already been on similar trips. My role in addition to being a paying passenger was that of voyage doctor. I only had to pay half the holiday fee by having this duty. After all, there had to be some incentive to take up the post of hospital doctor because I wouldn't do the job just for the love of it. I approached the role with slight trepidation and wondered whether it would affect my enjoyment of the trip. The fact of the matter was that I was supposed to be on holiday and not at work. Part of the reason to go on the trip was to escape work. Certainly, I didn't want an all-engrossing busman's holiday. Also, no one had better need urgent medical attention when up in the rigging. How on earth would I get up to them? Prayers would definitely be needed then. It was too late to get overly concerned about this, though, as there was no going back on what I had agreed to do.

The trip started in Gran Canaria from where we were sailing to other islands, the islands visited depending on the weather and the sea's behaviour. We managed to go to La Gomera and Tenerife during the week. The Lord Nelson is a Tall Ship with sails, rigging and so forth, which need to be manoeuvred by all onboard. It was a really hands-on trip and it certainly wasn't like a cruise, not that I've been on a cruise to compare. Us passengers were split into teams of ten and each team was put on different shifts with different responsibilities. Each team was given a member of the permanent crew as a leader. Fortunately, our team leader was quite laid back. We all wanted to get stuck into what needed to be done, but an over-enthusiastic leader would have made the trip less enjoyable. Everyone seemed to get on really well. People onboard seemed to like meeting other people and to enjoy a challenge. All those able managed to go up in the rigging to unfurl the sails when at sea. Even all willing wheelchair users were strapped in with the necessary ropes, winch and other equipment, and hoisted up to the first station on one of the masts when we were anchored in harbour midway through the trip. It was good fun, even if quite high, but thankfully done just the once. I could now appreciate how brave all those who had gone out on the yardarm at this height had been.

There was not a lot to see on the island of La Gomera. It was just good to put my wheels on solid ground after a couple of days at sea and it did feel quite strange not to be rocking up and down in time with the waves. After La Gomera and almost finding my land wheels again, we were next on land when we went to a beach by a dinghy powered by an outboard motor. We had to do it this way because the big boat could only come so close to shore when there was no harbour. There were several trips using the dinghy and only two wheelchairs could go in it with each trip to shore. It was really precarious being hoisted from the Tall Ship to the dinghy. The waves seemed all of a sudden to become the choppiest that they had been all week. Several people would be involved in the process of getting the wheelchair safely from the ship to the dinghy. The permanent crew had done this before……..I hoped!……and I just had to trust them, even though prayers did enter my head at the time.

When on the beach, I was helped down on to a towel. A couple of hours of lying in the sun, chatting, eating and drinking were enjoyed. It was good fun but very hot. I got badly scorched on the face despite having applied high sun factor protection cream. Being able to lie down out of the wheelchair was greatly enjoyed all the same. The wheelchair isn't the most comfortable thing to sit in. I would almost compare sitting in a wheelchair with standing up for someone without the paralysis affliction. When you're in a wheelchair, you don't get the opportunity to recline as you would in most other chairs. For someone who can walk, after a while the legs get tired and then it's a relief to get time to take a rest and sit down. Likewise, for someone in a wheelchair, after some time the back gets tired and then it's great to get a chance to rest by either sitting in a comfortable chair or lying down with legs out straight and back fully relaxed. Back to the beach experience. As well as being lifted down on to a beach towel, those of us unable to walk were carried into the sea to have a swim. It seemed almost like a religious show of baptism and thankfully the water was warm. Otherwise, I would have been out as quick as I went in. It was amazing how much more buoyant I was in the sea compared with a swimming pool. I didn't need to wave my arms at all to float on my back like I did when I was in a swimming pool. On this holiday we were doing so many things that I hadn't done in my new wheelchair life. I was also guaranteed to return from it looking healthy and fresh-faced, thanks to the salt water, wind and hot sun.

   Where did we go next? It was about day four of the holiday when we got to Tenerife. We had just made it there in our allotted time, which meant that we would have to turn back for Gran Canaria after a night on shore. It was a very well planned time to get to Tenerife because a festival was going on the night that we were there. It turned out to be a really good evening. Everyone left the boat as a possie out for fun. We mainly stuck together, stopping off at different bars, with interludes for dancing, listening to bands or whatever else grabbed the attention. I didn't fall out of my wheelchair, so I was obviously restrained and in control that night. The streets were packed with people and dancers, singers, jugglers and people in all sorts of colourful costumes were everywhere. A good party night indeed.

   Then it was back to Gran Canaria. Our team of ten was on nightwatch the night before finally mooring at Gran Canaria. We had to be at the wheel and to direct the ship according to the captain's instructions. It was such a still and quiet night and at about four in the morning a full moon could be seen on the horizon. The dark horizon was plain and empty, other than the white ball of the moon low down in the sky. All else that could be seen was the horizontal line separating sea from sky and the bright reflection of the moon seen glistening across the sea from horizon to boat in a trail of light. It was an amazing sight to behold as the perfectly round moon descended effortlessly below the distant water's edge. I watched the moon's fall to earth over about half an hour. It was so peaceful and I had never seen anything like this before. What a night! I didn't mind being awake at night when it was like that.

We arrived at Gran Canaria later that day. Our last night was on shore. We were going to have a good time out boozing before taking a two-hour trip by van the following afternoon to the airport. We went out in force and our proposed final destination that night was to be a British pub bar known to regular attenders. A good time was had in the pub, especially when Nick and I ended up in a nearby bar afterwards with two Norwegian women. They were extremely attractive and this was definitely not due to beer goggles. Even better, they were willing to keep up English-Norwegian relations. I was certainly all for that, too, but Nick was sadly unable to do such close negotiating between our two countries because he was Ellie's boyfriend. After initial negotiations, we headed back in the direction of the boat. It was a long way and being ever the gentleman, I had to insist that the one with who I had been doing most close negotiations sat on my lap to save her legs. She appreciated this as much as me. Then suddenly I had two on my lap and was being pushed at high speed. Bang! Off flew the Norwegians. My wheelchair had hit a kerb and one of the two small front wheels had shattered. Nick looked a bit sheepish having been the person who had done the pushing. It would have been a problem if it had been at the start of the holiday. We only had less than a day of it left and the wheelchair could still wheel, even if with a bit of a limp. I asked the Norwegian lady to sit on my lap on the side away from the damaged wheel to balance it out and she kindly cooperated. At about six in the morning, we finally arrived back at the boat and we reluctantly said goodbye to the Norwegians. As Nick and I got on the boat, people were beginning to get up and, after pretending that we were doing the same, we took a sneaky hour's snooze and then made it to breakfast at about eight.

What else had happened that night? Before we had got to the British pub bar, Nick had fallen into a ditch. Well, it was more like a small quarry. He was lucky not to hurt himself and he found it hard to get out of it, but finally managed after many attempts. Ellie had also had her adventures and my wheelchair front wheel had not been the only casualty. She and a vet onboard the ship had gone swimming in the sea in the early hours and she put her foot on a sea urchin resulting in its spikes being left behind in one of her feet. The vet had to be the doctor when they got back to the boat and he injected local anaesthetic to enable easier removal of the spikes. Fortunately, no one had been irreparably injured in this eventful night. It was one of the best that I've ever had, a real laugh and a half.

Overall, there were not too many casualties for the voyage doctor to assess. Admittedly, I didn't assess Ellie. Nonetheless, there was the ship's engineer who cut his finger on a broken glass bottle top before we set sail on the first day. This just needed an injection and a couple of stitches. Then there was someone with a sore throat and that was it. It turned out to be an easy way to have a half-price ticket. It had been a great trip away, an intrepid adventure with some stories for friends back home. I had had a really active holiday despite my wheelchair. There had been no obvious barriers to an excellent trip and I would have never imagined this possible a few years before. I had managed a challenging experience and most importantly very much enjoyed it. Good memories indeed.

Chapter 49

Now how did I get out of this dreadful mess?

I have probably repeated several points on a few occasions in this book. Why is this so? Surely not to put off the reader. That would be a mistake. Even the novice businessman in me can spot that. Is it that I cannot be bothered to get my messages succinctly into a tighter narrative? Not really. Instead I want to convey how I have had to struggle over and over thoughts in my head, to rationalise things, to figure out where I am going in my life and whether there is or should be a reason for what happened to me. So I apologise for going through my endless mind games, taking you through this turmoil. At the same time, though, you are welcome to mine if you feel that you have benefited from the experience.

There isn't a universal solution to the multiplicity of problems in life. I haven't produced a manual on how to live your life. Everyone has different problems with which to contend. I simply have some lessons from my experiences on which I and hopefully others can draw. There will have been even further good to come out of what has happened to me if this is the case. Support is one thing that I have kept going on about. I guess that I have had support from many different sources and there are certain people from whom support will always come. The support is resolute. In the same way, I hope that the mentioning of it in this book has been resolute. Knowing that there are people there for me is extremely strengthening.

Music, film and interacting with other people have been sources of insight and strength for me. I read part of a book, hear certain lyrics or reflect on an aspect of a film, and it can parallel with my life. It makes some of my experiences more understandable. It can encapsulate my thoughts so well by verbalising what I have only thought. A passage from a book "Message in a Bottle" by Nicholas Sparks conveyed to me how I approach each challenge in my life. It eloquently conveyed that you get strength from those important in your life, both living and dead. The important people in my life in many ways define me, even after their deaths.

You do not have to have religious faith to think this. You simply have to feel that people who have been and are close to you have a presence with you in your life. At different times, you draw strength from memories of them. There is one particular thing that I want to tell my family, especially my parents. It isn't something that can be said casually in passing conversation. Luckily, the protection in the protracted nature of a book's conception permits it to be said without embarrassment or haste. They have truly shaped my life and dramatically for the positive. They have literally made my life possible. They are part of me and I am eternally grateful for their wonderful presence. The emotions expressed are by their nature deeply felt. I do indeed owe these people my life and they will always be a special part of me. They are dearly loved by me. Thank you for loving me.

I have listed the many sources of strength and with it hope during my traumatic hospital experience and beyond:
- people by my bedside, even when I didn't acknowledge their presence on all occasions: just knowing people were there gave me a feeling that I was wanted in this life;
- nursing staff and allied professionals who treated me like a person helped me keep my sense of worth: physically altered but mentally much the same;
- my parents and siblings being ever optimistic, bringing my and in a way their home to hospital when I was there for so long: a time when every little bit of positivity is needed to mould your attitude to make the most of your situation;
- waking up from my neck operation to catch my mother's blue eyes of support and concern, as she read a book at my bedside: I was not in this dreadful situation alone;
- the doctors' empathy with my condition and wish to improve my situation, especially with regard to my lost voice and tracheostomy tube;
- the spirit and collective humour of the other spinally-injured patients;
- my dad's continual and unsuccessful efforts to try to understand me when I could only mouth words: he did so much to help me and my

frustration at him not being able to understand me was sometimes uncalled for in view of all that he did;
- the tolerance of friends and family of my mood, my mood not always being good but rarely, if ever, criticised;
- faith: important for me as a source of strength and for much of my life's purpose, but I don't want this book to be seen as purely an evangelical crusade;
- the medical school fundraising and support;
- the past experiences that I could look back on when feeling down: made especially apparent when I listened to a tape one evening in hospital on which three friends had recorded their voices and it made me forget my situation for a vital period.

  This is sounding like an Academy Awards speech. I don't think that I am a particularly special person. In any case, what is the meaning of special? Is it kind, strong, honest, diligent? I don't exactly know. The interpretation of language by different people can vary greatly. Language and communication is complicated and mixed messages can occur. It's often difficult to get the right words, although sometimes it doesn't matter just as long as people can get the gist of what you're meaning. At least a long book is a good way to give a broad impression of many issues. Back to special. I think that people can be special to each other. I think that people can be said to have achieved amazing things, but even so this doesn't really help with my definition of special. I don't think that it matters, though. What am I trying to say? Perhaps it's to say that opportunities as well as a person's motivation determine what a person achieves.

  There are many people in my life who I think are special to me, probably more in number as a result of my accident. I do admittedly have determination, but this has been inspired by people's generosity and willing for good to happen along the way. The message is that hope is the key. People gain it from many different sources. Discover it and life can be a joyful experience for many people. I feel saddened for people that don't find it. Thank you to all of those that have helped me find mine. Why have I kept repeating thank yous in this book? Some people would say that I have been almost sycophantic, but it's not meant to be sycophantic. I simply feel the need to let people know how much I have valued and do value their support. It's meant to be sincere and a book is a lasting vehicle for my appreciation. How can I describe the love and generosity that I was given and felt during my experience? How can I explain an emotion? I can't. I have simply experienced it. It's as difficult as communicating a religious belief or something intimately personal. It's not easily definable. No words can express it fully, but I hope that this book has communicated it to some extent. What has happened has happened and I hope that those involved know that I often remember my experience of human kindness.

  My accident was in some way a lot worse for my family, especially in the initial stages. I was simply trying to stay alive and unaware of a lot that was happening, whereas my poor family and close friends must have been very aware of the situation. It is plainly apparent to me now that this particular time must have been very difficult for them and I can only imagine how it must have been for them. You and your family work through the tough times in the early aftermath and sink or swim, live or die. Phrases like "no pain, no gain," "you don't struggle, there's no progress," and "when the going gets tough, the tough….." are aimed at getting you through the difficult times. Even though you feel like swearing at these phrases, they do have some truth. Unless you push yourself, you will rarely achieve new goals. If it wasn't worth it, you probably wouldn't strive for it.

  The accident and all the things that have happened are now memories lessening with time. The long-term consequences of what has happened are what remain. That's why they're called long-term after all. It is the permanency of my injuries that is at the crux of the issue for me now. The long-standing problems are grinding on the personality and a certain amount of motivation is needed to contend with them. Life is more of a struggle with a long-term impairment, but it is necessary to get on with life and not dwell on the past and new impairments. Life is for the living and for sharing with others, rather than unproductively mourning the past, and having survived I can now thankfully do a bit of living and sharing with others.

  Two very important people for me to continue to share life with are my parents. Often I consciously reaffirm my appreciation of them by asking myself, "How come I've got such fantastic parents? Why am I so lucky?" They have been unerring in their support along the way. I hope that I have given a bit back to them by trying to make the most of my opportunities and to want to be close to them and to help in any way. They deserve so much praise and recognition for being such generous people. Some of it comes from me here. They have been truly amazing. Other family members and friends are also valued in my eyes. It's been a long haul of adjustment for many people along the way. There have been no quick fixes, but it has been made much easier by having a lot of caring people who have each contributed a helping hand in one way or another.

     My mum said on one occasion that she would give anything for me to have my legs back as before. She even said that she would give me her legs, that she would trade places. I appreciate her love and the desire to change things for me and she knows that I do. Nevertheless, always one to find the funny side of things, I commented, "What? Two arthritic ones and each with an artificial hip?" to a chorus of our laughter. And I wasn't avoiding a sensitive issue in a typically male way. Instead we knew how much we cared for each other's welfare and this shared humour made us even closer. My mum would do almost anything for her family, as would my dad. So would I. Love between people is infinitely more important and fulfilling than physical abilities. Generosity of spirit is a fantastic thing to give and receive. If only it could be more prevalent in the world. The feature film "Pay it forward" idealises the significance of doing this by passing on good deeds received to other people. It was badly reviewed by the critics on the Ceefax pages of the television, but I thought it was a great film. Go and see it to judge who's the best critic. Probably not the naïve film watcher and sentimentalist Wells. I like to dream about a more perfect world, full of kindness. Let me have that privilege.

Chapter 50

Where am I now?

No, I'm not hallucinating again! What I really mean is: where am I in my life? It is now the year 2000 and I am still working as a doctor and still enjoying life. I have now worked as a hospital doctor for four and a half years. I am trying to get a job in which I train and specialise in cancer medicine.

I don't feel that I have made any major mistakes in my choices since my accident. There is nothing that sticks out where I wished that I hadn't done it. I very much enjoy working as a doctor and I probably have a lot to offer. This could sound like a job interview if I'm not careful. The career path through medicine can be unsettling at times and choices often have to be made between location, specialty, family commitments and so forth. Ideally I would like to stay in the same area of the country because I like it where I am and I would like to stay near my family. Also I feel a bit more restricted in that it is harder for me to find suitable housing, with the need for it to be accessible if I were to move. The specialist posts can be few and far between and most of the posts last five years with you staying in a designated region of the country for that time. So I'm biding my time, as I wait for a post to be advertised near to the South West region. It's important to keep different options open, though, and create more pies for my fingers, so I'm also trying to sort out some research. Who knows whether it will all go swimmingly? I have to be prepared to change if that is necessary. The important thing is that I am working now and I am well qualified to have an interesting job, even if it doesn't end up being my first choice of specialty.

I had better steer away from work before I make you lose interest. How can I spice things up, though? Should I let you know all the scandal? I won't go quite that far, but one question to spice things up might be whether I am in an intimate relationship. No, I am not at the moment. There have been some since of varying duration since my accident, but I've not had one longer than nine months. Perhaps I don't want to deal with the consequences of pregnancy. No, I don't think that I'm a father yet. There is probably more baggage brought along with me because of my paralysis condition, but I tend to be an easy-going bloke despite life's apparent analysis in this book. Now what I'm writing sounds more like a dating advertisement rather than a job interview. Perhaps one of my next goals should be to break the nine-month barrier. Fortunately, I'm wise enough about relationships to know that this wouldn't work. My experience tells me that directly you start setting expectations on relationships, especially without the other person agreeing, they usually break down. So maybe it won't be a goal, after all.

There are some things that I miss within the context of intimacy: close dancing and hand-in-hand walking are to name a couple. I often used to look with sad envy at couples walking along holding hands, although this sadness has faded a bit. I can dance in my imagination, though, and I have to find alternative ways to these to express intimacies. Fortunately, there are many surrogates to these actions and I wonder whether for that reason I am being greedy wanting those things missed. I don't think so. We all should be allowed to grieve for things lost. Why on earth am I worried about it, though, when I'm not even in a relationship at the moment? Just don't give me tablets for it, doc, because I'm not that bad yet. It's controlled and probably rational grief and I've managed to get on with my life despite appreciating this loss for a few years now. I sound now like I'm trying to convince the doctor that I'm not unstable. Honestly, my spirit is buoyant, even if my legs have no strength.

People might read this book and think that I have not revealed enough of my secrets despite its length. I certainly feel that I have managed to communicate things honestly and in the way that I have experienced and approached them. I think that I have revealed a lot of my inner self, probably more than most people would be comfortable doing. There is in fact very little unsaid. The things about which my close acquaintances and I don't talk don't matter. They are mainly the awful and intricate details of the accident. We all know how bad it had been and we are aware of each other's appreciation of it. There is no need to go over it again. We are also aware of how lucky things turned out after such a horrific accident. That appreciation of me being alive far outshines any badness that occurred, almost to make it insignificant. I really don't think that I'm overstating it in saying that my presence here is almost like a miracle.

There have been ups and downs. All that I know is where I am now, a little about where I would like to be headed and the rest of the time is preoccupied with the hustle and bustle of my life like most other folk. However, I try not to get too preoccupied. Thumbs up to rest and relaxation, time for contemplation; just as long as I don't get too boring about my reflections. Otherwise, people might say, "Oh goodness. Here comes that tedious bloke. He's always analysing everything. Why can't he just chill out and enjoy himself? Let's make a sharp exit." Life is for living after all and preferably with mates and a few laughs along the way.

Despite this, my amateur philosophy continues. Life is idiosyncratic or individualistic depending on which word you would prefer to use. What people want, value and strive for can be very different. Genetic preservation, thrill, security and enjoyment are to name a few; some are conscious, others subconscious. I think that it is safe to say, though, that most want some sort of contentment. I wonder if that statement is patronising and so blindingly obvious that it need not be said. A cliché phrase goes, "Life is a journey and you don't know exactly where it will take you." That is the interesting part of life. How is it possible for someone to know what will fulfil them in future years? It's purely guesswork. They can only know whether they are fulfilled in the present. However someone feels, I don't believe that they can ever be completely fulfilled. One simply has to reach a happy medium. It's human nature to complain and have some dissatisfaction, as well as having the opposite emotions. If one never has bad times, one doesn't appreciate the good ones. I have discovered a lot about myself on my trip so far and I think that I have come away a better person from all my experiences. I shall keep wandering on my path and it is still good not to know exactly where the path is going. What a bore it would be to have no surprises. I like life being a dynamic experience with many unanswered questions and challenges to be tackled, as well as times to enjoy. I wouldn't want it to be any different.

I have now come full circle. The memories of hospital life as a patient seem distant and will fade even further with time. I'm still asking questions. How should I end this book? Should I finish convincing the reader that I have achieved all my dreams? Certainly not. Even so, at least I am somewhere on the way to a few of them. We all need hope and opportunities in our lives. "You make your own luck" has some truth in it. Some people on the other hand believe in fate. "Que sera sera: what will be will be" echoes true in that case. I do, however, feel that many of your chances are created by those around you. In any case, whether or not this is fate can be debated endlessly. The people around you are governed to a large extent by the relationships that you forge in life; but, there again, your family and situations to meet people are generally presented to you by chance. Serendipity is a slightly more flowery word. Perhaps I should use it to sell this book to those wanting to read complicated language. No, chance is a good enough word. Whatever words I use, the debate about fate or no fate is a bit of a circular and irrelevant one. I simply want to convey messages, not to impress the reader with beautiful language. I feel, though, that what I and other people do does matter, irrespective of whether or not fate exists. We need to try to live a good earthly life, whether it be for religious or other reasons.

    Dare I mention religion? Sadly, religion can be a taboo word. With today's hectic lifestyles, people rarely get time to relax, let alone consider things such as religion. People get labeled as fish positive and other slightly critical terms if they are religious. It is a hard thing to communicate what being religious encompasses to those who don't have religious beliefs. Being a very personal thing, it is rightly difficult to express what you feel to someone who doesn't have a similar belief. Even people who have a religious belief express it in a different way. They can also have different beliefs. It is the unknown, I suppose, that makes it so elusive to many. My beliefs have always been there, but I had not given a commitment to my faith until relatively recently when I was confirmed. I don't wear religion on my sleeve, but being confirmed was an important thing for me to do to show a certain commitment. It was something which I always considered doing in my late-teens and early-twenties, but I had never made time for it. After my release from hospital, I was lucky enough to have a Deacon at my local village church visit me regularly to have discussions about religion and what it meant to me. This was very valuable and I was privileged to have this undivided attention. Religion is important to me and getting confirmed was important in my personal religious development. It indeed needs to develop continually, as my life goes on. It has deepened me as a person to have been confirmed and now to be allowed to participate in communion. I have to put my life's motives in perspective and not to think just of me, me, me. I think that I would have probably not made the time to be confirmed, had my life not slowed down as a result of my accident, and this would have been a mistake. It's strange how opportunities present themselves. It is exciting to develop as a person in different ways, whether it is work, leisure, faith or whatever may present itself in life.

    Occasionally I used to attend meetings of fellow confirmation candidates. These were valuable sessions to hear other people's views and experiences and you can learn so much from talking and most importantly listening to other people. We would sometimes be given exercises to do. This could be a little scary because it often involved revealing personal aspects of your life and things that you didn't really want to tell others. A lot could be learned from these exercises, difficult as they were. One day we each had to draw a tree that represented our life. Mine had a broken branch damaged by lightening, but it also had firm roots. The tree was still standing. In this picture I could see the most terrible event in my life so far, while at the same time appreciative of the strong support that had prevented the tree from falling. The devastating event had not uprooted the tree. It stood and there was life from which to continue to grow and develop. The branch was dead and wouldn't be recovered. In the same way some part of my earlier life had died, not to be recovered in its entirety. But this was only part of my life. It did not prevent the tree or my life from blooming and becoming a beautiful thing. The dead branch and memory of what had been lost in my life would whither and lessen in size with time, as the tree's growth continued.

    I am certainly not going to give up on this life despite having had my past traumas. I almost have less of a reason to give up than someone who hasn't been through an experience such as mine. Although I appear to have lost a great deal by becoming paralysed, I have gained so much by almost dying but having not done so. Having been so close to death, I know more than ever that you have to grasp life and rejoice in living it to the full. If ever I feel that I need some reminding of this, the song "Don't give up" by Kate Bush and Peter

Gabriel plays in my mind and gives me strength to continue the battle called life. My life goes on and there is much to gain from it. Music, friends and faith are some of many supports.

Close dancing was mentioned earlier as something lost. I am indeed dancing in my head despite my obvious outward losses. I would hope that this optimism and contentment with life is apparent when people meet me. Music is incredibly empowering for me. The joy about music for me is in its effortlessness for the user. I can simply put a song on the stereo and let the words float into my head. So many messages can be heard, so many reinforcers to what I have thought. Also there doesn't necessarily have to be a message. It can just be good to listen to, relaxing or get me in the mood that I want. I have certainly used it, both listening to it as I write this book and referring to some songs in parts of the book. If I used every track that has inspired me, the book would be much longer. Relief all round that I didn't then! And believe it or not, even though I might waffle on at times, I do actually want to finish writing this book. Nevertheless, another song that has inspired me is "I hope you dance" by Lee Ann Womack. She sings of dancing with the meaning of grasping opportunities and recognising the wonder of life, whatever happens along the way. At least this is what I think she is doing and, if so, it has certainly inspired me to dance.

Chapter 51

Closing thoughts: the end is near

How do I describe the experience of almost dying? I cannot adequately do so. All that can be said is that I now have a personal familiarity of being at death's door. Implicit in this is death being less of a mystery and less scary. It is difficult to say how you feel about something unless you have experienced it and I suppose that by almost experiencing death that I can more easily know how I feel about it. The calmness that I felt when almost dying of asphyxia due to my windpipe narrowing has reassured me. It did not turn out to be my time to die and the sensation of imminent death had not been a scary experience. Somehow it made me calm about everything else that lay and that still lies ahead for me. My faith in being able to get through virtually anything in life is now unerring. In fact, nothing really scares me greatly about life now and that is probably because the ultimate anxiety, namely dying, is no longer one. I am truly blessed to have this unique perspective on life.

    The feeling of peace when almost dying must have partly resulted from me being happy with the way that my life had been conducted up to that point. There were no regrets other than wanting to continue living. I need to keep trying to live a just life so that the next time that I am at death's door, there will again be no regrets tainting the experience. I want to feel the same pleasant experience when death comes for me again and I feel that this should happen if I continue to strive for a worthy life. Although I would rather not die quite yet, it is very comforting to have a secure feeling about one's own mortality. It is probably one of the major mental strengths that I now have. I feel like I have been given a second chance at this life and I can appreciate it more than ever, which is why I want to get on with the enjoyment of living, to fulfil life's potential and to let people know my story.

    Each day is appreciated more than before. Never again should I moan on about some petty issue continuously. Sometimes moaning can make you feel better, but there is a limit to it and to people's tolerance of a moody person. Do things for change, for a purpose, for kindness, for enjoyment and interest, but not just simply to moan. Let there be many more days, mainly because I like being alive. Rather selfish of me; probably not. There's so much possible to do in life that I don't want to waste my time over pointless things. I want to make the most of the gifts that I have been given. I hear a heckler cry out, "Well, writing ain't one of your talents, so please stop. At least don't waste your time with a second book." It's good to question your own capabilities and sometimes you do need some third party advice. Even so, hate mail letters will not be appreciated. Critics are likely to dig their elbows in, so I had better do so first. My deliberate self-derision can be an all too frequent way to anticipate criticism and lessen its impact, especially when it isn't wanted. It's usually protective, but no matter how hard I try to self-criticise I secretly have high hopes of acclaim for this particular writing venture of mine. Whatever criticism may come my way, it's important for me to remind myself that the main objective has been to communicate with those close to me rather than literary or financial success.

 My period of being mute gave me an ideal opportunity to assess my situation and to reflect on how fortunate I had been with my opportunities in life. When you cannot talk to people, you have a lot of time to think. It made me appreciate that I have the most fantastic family and friends, both loyal and fun. My voice was gifted back to me by surgery and by good fortune that the procedures were successful. I have also had all the help needed since then to achieve my goals thus far. Now I have a job that I find enjoyable and challenging, a roof over my head and I am able to put these things into perspective by having an intimate understanding of life at extremes.

 It's not an ideal life path, but when I think of all these good things, it somehow makes my paralysis seem less significant. Life is often unfair and someone can be muted and disadvantaged through bad luck, by being prejudged by outsiders and by simply not being given opportunities. I hope in my daily life that I can be open-minded to people's capabilities and educate others to be likewise. We all have our preconceptions and prejudices. We will make mistakes, but hopefully we learn from them. It would be good if most people could be fair, even if life is not. Luckily, I have met many fair and generous people. That's probably why I haven't been really angry about what has happened to me, when others have wondered how it is possible to be anything but angry. I guess that forgiveness and getting on with purposeful activities has helped me have a positive outlook. Not being angry and instead directing my energy positively has been very healthy for me and my outlook on life.

Everyone has hidden aspects to their personality and general make-up. When you meet someone, you do not tell him or her all of your achievements and perceived strengths. That would be thought of as rather strange and also pretty arrogant. There are items behind the curtains of everyone's outward exterior. It can be especially misleading or hard to gauge someone's potential when the individual being scrutinised is put in an unfamiliar situation. A person's personality and capabilities can be very occult and elusive for even the individual themselves to find at stressful times. I try to take home the message that one should not judge on first impressions and outward appearances. These can be important, but they can often lead to prejudice and as a result be wrong. It takes a long time to know someone well. It even takes a long time to get to know yourself. Get rid of or at least recognise your assumptions and prejudice as much as you can. George Michael manages to remind me of this in his song "Waiting" from his "Listen without Prejudice" album.

Recognise your own faults and you'll probably view those of others more tolerantly. Give people the freedom and opportunities to express themselves at their own speed, and fairness and justice will at least have a better chance to prevail. Your thoughts as much as your actions define you as a person. My accident, resultant impairments and experiences have circumscribed choices that I have made. I feel that I have ended up a much better person than I probably would have been without my accident and its repercussions, despite the obvious impairments that remain. Life has taught me so much in such a short time. It's far better to live life as a fool and an optimist, rather than living it as a pessimist and being proved right when things go badly. You'll enjoy life more and people also tend to prefer happy and positive people.

I don't want to be thought of as a sad reminder of things lost. Definitely not. I want to be a glad reminder that spirit, humour, happiness, strength, love and support can make you look beyond the sadness to a valuable life that has become stronger rather than lost, and that this undying optimistic spirit has spread to affect others in a positive way. Spinal cord injury is a devastating occurrence: decreased mobility, continence problems, fertility issues, physical pain and other problems. It is not, however, the end of life. The adaptation process tends to be a continuum, a long journey with an uncertain ending. Tragedy spills into grief, grief changes to sad reflection, and sad reflection somehow becomes a secret strengthened resolve which is almost outwardly apparent. The damaged person who has adapted in a positive way can often seem to have something that most others don't, and that is a wisdom and undeniable perspective with which to tackle life and its challenges.

    I don't want to forget what has been done for me. Even if I become arrogant, "or more so" I hear you say, and forget about these experiences, at least this book can be a continuing testament of them and of how much I have valued all the help along the way. It is not simply a story of a man who had a life-changing event happen and his adapting to its consequences. When I chatted with someone about the book, she said that perhaps I had two books to write rather than just one. One would be about my recovery from hospital to home and the other could be about my reflections on life and what had happened. I felt that this wasn't possible because the two feel inseparable to me. As part of adjusting to my situation and getting out of hospital, I had to think in depth about where I was in my life, what I wanted, what life was all about and so forth in order to move on. That's why it is written so. You can learn the manoeuvres in rehabilitation to be as physically independent as possible, but that's only the half of it. You have to get your new life in your head somehow. It's not an easy thing to do and it takes a long time. It probably took me about four years before I reached a relatively steady state, both physically and mentally. I know that I've certainly adapted further since then. I was even in a wheelchair in one of my dreams a couple of months ago. I think that this was the first time it happened and the dream wasn't particularly memorable other than the fact that I was in a wheelchair. I can just remember straining as I reached up from my wheelchair to grab my brother's attention. It was outside my house's front door. I can't remember anything more than that about the dream. Analyse that. I find it funny how the body and mind work sometimes, with or without analysis.

"Do I want to be cured of the long-lasting impairments that have remained?" is an interesting question to which most people would think the answer would be, "Of course I do." I think that early on I grasped at trying to change things in the context of cure. I had some reflexology sessions in which my feet and hands were rubbed in different places to affect different organs of the body. This didn't cure me, but it was pleasant to have. Then I went to a spiritual healer and had laying on of hands. I didn't have to travel all the way to Lourdes for this because the spiritual healer visited was just outside central Bristol: far cheaper to get to. I must say that I did have a peculiar warm sensation throughout my body when the laying on of hands was done. I only went the one time and it was to no avail. Life seemed to have no obvious logic in the way that unfairness was delegated to people and that's why it was my hope that these unconventional measures might help cure my problem when conventional measures had little to offer in terms of cure.

It will be interesting to see how treatment progresses in this field of medicine and to see if people can be cured of spinal cord injury in more conventional ways. Naturally it is intriguing for me to see treatments develop in an area of medicine that integrally affects me. Importantly, though, I have not needed a cure to get on with my life. The prospect of cure hasn't been needed for my recovery. After all, recovery is not everything returning to what it previously was. It's about developing a worthwhile life for myself. I probably wouldn't reject a cure, though, if one came along. However, it's best for me not to be cured before this book is published. Highly unlikely, that is cure of spinal cord injury rather than book publication, although I don't know a great deal about the difficulties and challenge of getting a book published yet. Nevertheless, cure is not all that simple for several reasons. Firstly, it will be difficult to achieve. Secondly, if my physical problem were cured, it would still not take away all that has happened to me. Whatever happens, I wouldn't want that and that's because my life has been permanently changed for the better in many ways.

People have commented on the calm and almost detached way in which I recount what has happened to me. I certainly don't want to trivialise aspects of my experience by seeing the bright side of things, even though this has helped me retain my sanity. It would be a shame if this has disguised how truly devastating the events were that have occurred. There's no getting away from it. It was a dreadfully awful ordeal with which to contend. How can I say that it is not hard for a very fit man with a prosperous future ahead of him to have a shocking accident and many physical capabilities taken away in a split second? This included many injuries at the accident scene, luck not to die on more than one occasion, more than ten operations in a year, inability to speak from windpipe scarring, paralysis from the chest down and the list goes on. The struggle, and struggle it has been, has been long and challenging; but I have not been on my own. I have had amazing support. Some people are not so fortunate in their opportunities. Now, after all that, my future looks like it could be prosperous again, but it could so easily have been different. There are many ifs and buts along our life paths and I hope that I don't forget the privilege of having choices.

  The secret is to take positives from things, rather than dwelling on the negatives. The glass is half-full, not half-empty. Despite the occasional expletives of "bloody" throughout my narrative, I have no hatred or animosity against anyone or anything that happened. The expression of "bloody" by me has often been a way of releasing frustration and it is usually said in a tongue-in-cheek manner. It has probably been used rather liberally and its use had better not undermine me as an angry bitter person. That would be a mistake if it has, and I feel a misrepresentation of me. Forgiving and even sometimes forgetting bad experiences tends to be a better philosophy. It can occasionally be hard to do that, but it's very unproductive to hold grudges. It doesn't help anyone, either grudger or grudgee. Hey, I think I've invented a new word or two. Who's ever heard of a grudgee? Never mind; bygones! It's far better to look to the future and to be generous towards people and their intentions. After all, life is primarily for the living and secondarily for the reflection. One shouldn't dwell obsessively on future dreams and past things behind, and in the process forget to live. Often both reflection and living are necessarily interlinked. Reflection can be a very positive thing but it can also be negative, and one has to be ever alert to it suffocating the act of getting on with the living. I'm pretty sure that one knows when the right balance between living and reflection has been achieved. I think that I have reached a steady balance and it doesn't feel that bad. In fact, I would be bold enough to say that it's fairly good. Who knows if it could be much better?

I've had some unlucky things happen to me, yet feel lucky in many ways. I have fantastic friends and family, probably realised more now than before all this adventure started. I also have a job which I enjoy, a comfortable home, enough money to enjoy the occasional holiday and my medical condition could have been a lot worse. When thinking about it, I am more than likely better off in my life than many people. Also, reflecting on the positives further, it had been possible to operate on my windpipe, the windpipe operations themselves were successful, I have no lasting brain damage and most of all I am alive. I am alive. I bloody well am alive! I can't scream on paper. Who cares? Let's have a go. I am bloody alive (scream)! I am bloody alive (scream louder)! I enjoy and value my life more than ever.

I would like to think that my writing has been valued by those close to me, although in the book there are probably painful memories for some people. I do hope that I have not upset anyone too much and that important messages contained in the story have made it all worthwhile. Friends and family have been my invaluable advocates. They were there for me in many ways: hands to hold, faces to see, voices when mine couldn't be heard, unquestioning support and non-judgemental attitudes, fundraisers for my future and people to remember when at low points. The strength from their friendship still remains by simply having them in my memory. Apologies, thanks and love are from me for those involved.

A life can be profoundly damaged in a moment, but it can be rebuilt in years to something even stronger than before. Opportunity, support, determination, belief, patience and self-reflection are paramount to success in the eyes of the affected. There are so many aspects to life's fulfilment. Who knows what I will want to do next? Whatever that may be, what's more important is that where I am now in life is more than I could ever have envisaged. For most of the time, I was unsure whether I would be able to achieve my next goal. Sometimes it would just happen. I was given the opportunities for this trial and error game of life achievement. There was indeed much possibility in me after my accident and I have certainly surprised myself by what I have managed to do.

Possibility is essential for all of us. It is what our game of life achievement is all about. Without it, there is no hope or ambition. Set no limits to what can be achieved. Even more good will come from my life if my story helps to inspire others to realise their dreams. Indeed, when we let our own light shine, we somehow give others the permission to do the same.

THE END

....................OR IS IT SIMPLY ANOTHER BEGINNING?

I completed writing this book more than 5 years ago. Now it is 2006 and I have a wonderful wife Mary and a beautiful daughter Lily Florence Wells. Wow! I am a husband and a dad. After becoming paralysed, I had grieved thinking that I would never be able to be a dad. Life is a truly amazing thing. I realise its beauty more than ever and not naïvely. There will be difficulties and traumas ahead. However, I take life as it comes and appreciate the very good things rather than being beaten up by the bad. Beating my disability has not been about a medical cure. Instead it has been about realising life's many opportunities. What a wonderful life.

Printed in Great Britain
by Amazon